THE RA
RI

MW00619676

ALLAGASH TAILS VOL. VII
TALES FROM
MAINE'S NATIONAL WILD
AND SCENIC RIVER

Written by

Tim Caverly

Illustrated by

Franklin Manzo, Jr.

Edited by
Nancy's Proofreading, Lewiston, Maine
njsm@roadrunner.com

Copyright pending © 2016 by Tim Caverly
Illustrations copyright © by Franklin Manzo, Jr.
Allagash Tails LLC 2016
Millinocket, Maine
Library of Congress Cataloging-in-Publication Data
Caverly, Tim.
Allagash Tails: A Collection of Stories from Maine's "Wild and Scenic River"
Vol. VII:
The Ranger and the Reporter
Written by Tim Caverly
Illustrated and compiled by Franklin Manzo, Jr.
P.cm.-(wildlife)

Summary: This is the seventh book in the Allagash Tails collection. The story: a cub reporter has been assigned to interview a retired Maine Park Ranger who spent years in the Allagash woods. The man, waiting out his final days in a nursing home, is famous for being illusive and secretive. Others haven't been able to break through his resistance to get their story. Tag along with our lady journalist as she struggles to unearth the real life experiences of a wilderness ranger and in the process; learns there is more to a person's life than waiting for an inscription on a tombstone, even hers.

ISBN #978-1-4951-9960-8
Printed in the U.S.A.

The paper in this book is FSC® Forest Stewardship Council® certified and all production was done with 100% wind power.

First Printing, March, 2016

DEDICATION

To the family of Wayne Harper

My good friend, Wayne Harper, of Presque Isle, Maine was an educator, guide, historian, and purveyor of many philosophical discussions and practical experiences. (Sometimes he'd lead theoretical discussions about such subjects as the Icelandic Monetary System about which neither of us had any knowledge.)

Perhaps the proper way to devote a work to a person best described as a northern Maine renaissance man, is to share an excerpt from his personal journals. The following was found in a log book that he'd kept one winter while we were on an overnight snowmobile camping trip at Ziegler campsite in the Allagash Wilderness Waterway:

Before we turned in for the night, I rode my sled to [Eagle] lake. Once there, on that vast, dark, ghostly quiet, expanse of empty snow and ice I parked my sled in the middle, rested my head on the handle bars, put my feet up on the seat back and absorbed the spectacular show of the heavens. If you have never seen the night sky from the wilderness, you have surely missed one of life's wonderful gifts. Big bright stars, millions and millions! In the far distance I can faintly hear the cry of an owl; in the nearer distance is the bark of a coyote. As I look and listen, deep thoughts of philosophy fill my mind; life, space, creation, ending, hopes, future, and above all, how insignificant I really am! At that moment, I really missed Tim. He and I could have really done some fine philosophy this night!

   We dedicate this book to the Harper family and the ideals that Wayne and his wife Sylvia practice every day, ethical standards which recognized the significance of natural experiences, our historical heritage and the necessity of sharing and preserving them for others.

Tim Caverly
Franklin Manzo, Jr.
Millinocket, Maine 04462
March 2016

PREAMBLE

Happy 100th Birthday National Park Service

Happy 50th Anniversary

Allagash Wilderness Waterway

Anyone who studies the history of our national parks and wild and scenic rivers will discover multitudes of controversy that stormed over efforts to protect our special areas. While thousands appreciate the opportunity to recharge in the outdoors, there are a few who argue for development to the detriment of the environment.

The efforts to preserve the Allagash began early and have lasted for years. In July of 1961 the Federal Government proposed an Allagash National Riverway and the establishment of a 300,000-acre recreational area.

In 1963, a Maine Allagash Advisory Committee was established and the working group conducted public meetings and recommended compromises. Due to the committee's efforts, 68% of Maine voters approved, in 1966, a referendum for a $1.5-million bond issue, an amount when passed, was matched by the Federal Bureau of Outdoor Recreation. This vote was citizens' approval for the establishment of the Allagash Wilderness Waterway, an area where there is to be "development of maximum wilderness character."

But the creation of Maine's now treasured wilderness experience did not come easy and without debate. One dispute was over a dam that would have flooded 97% of the river. A bi-product of the Passamaquoddy Tidal Project, the Rankin Rapids impoundment on the St. John River was proposed to supplement the tidal plan. If built, the dam would have flooded upstream from Allagash Village to Eagle Lake.

Thankfully the efforts to build the dam failed and bids to protect the area continued. In a dedication ceremony on July 19, 1970, Senator Ed Muskie proclaimed the inclusion of the Allagash into the National Park Service's Wild and Scenic River System. The first such state- administrated *wild river* in the United States.

Today we have a state-managed wilderness area that people from all over world come to visit. But is the state's administration of the Waterway perfect?

In retrospect the corridor may have been better preserved under federal control—perhaps a national canoe route would have been less susceptible to local whims. (Since 1966 Maine legislators have introduced and/or enacted over 40 pieces of legislation to deal with a variety of agendas.)

But, despite all of the challenges, the Waterway experience works. And it works because of the many who care for the natural experience found between "the banks." But I expect there will always be challenges to keeping our natural areas in perpetuity. When it comes to money, there are many who would exploit for profit; without consideration, it seems, for the economic benefit that many communities enjoy from neighboring national recreational areas.

I was Ranger Supervisor of the AWW in 1991 when the Waterway's 25 birthday was celebrated at Churchill Dam. At the time, the Director of the Bureau of Parks rededicated the state's efforts to manage the Allagash as a wild river.

2016 marks the 50th anniversary of the Waterway and the 100th birthday of both the National Park Service and Acadia National Park.

As our nation celebrates the prudence that conserved our natural treasures, treat yourself. Explore our great Acadia, paddle the fabulous Allagash, and sing Happy Birthday to both. Your life will be changed for the better.

Hope I am around for the cake at their next anniversary.

Tim Caverly
Millinocket, Maine
March 2016

A PERSON'S LABORS OF TODAY
MAY NOT SERVE THE TRIALS OF
TOMORROW!
A MISSION IN LIFE CAN ONLY BE
UNDERSTOOD;
UPON THE DISCOVERIES OF THE
MORROW

James P. Clark
Pleasant Ridge
Assisted Living Community

ACKNOWLEDGEMENTS

Frank and I wish to extend our appreciation for the support, encouragement and assistance to the many that helped with our story.

Without their aid this portrayal of the north woods would not have been possible. Our deepest gratitude to Bean's Eye Photography, Dean Bennett, Donat and Harriet Busque, Roger Currier, Sylvia Harper, Terry Harper, David Hubley, Joan King, Matt LaRoche, Nancy Moyer, Rod and Stella Flewelling, and Mark Woodward.

And to our wives, Susan Caverly and Sara Manzo, for puttin' up with our antics while we worked days, nights, and weekends to bring this story to you.

Enjoy!

Tim Caverly
Franklin Manzo Jr.

Millinocket, Maine
March 2016

PREFACE

My grandfather Lester Stevens had a reputation!

He was quick witted—Ulysses Grant [aka Lester] Stevens lived on Hilton Hill in Cornville, Maine. He married late in life and wedded a young Alice Getchell, 20 years his junior. When asked why he waited so long to complete his nuptials Lester replied, "Well, if I get a good wife, I will be well paid for waiting. If I got a poor wife, I will have long enough to live with her."

This is only one example of my grandfather's sense of humor and is probably where my brother Buzz and I inherited our pleasure of sharing adventures. Often my mom would say that her dad, a dedicated member of the Grange and Masons, would entertain whenever called upon or when an opportunity arose, whether the audience occurred at a scheduled meeting or whenever a bunch of folks informally gathered at a local hardware store.

He loved children—Lester and Alice had four children and he valued their company, no matter what he was doing. Two sons and two daughters, his youngest daughter, my mom Pauline (Polly), told me that when she was too young to walk in the woods my grandfather would carry her in a pack basket until they reached a favorite trout hole so my mom could fish with him.

My mom's brother and my uncle, John Alden, tells how—at a very young age—he'd ride for hours in the lap of his dad, cutting field grass while the farm's horse and hay rake did their work.

I remember visiting my Republican grandfather when very young; a time when he suffered terribly from Parkinson disease. An illness so debilitating that the sickness caused the once rugged man to spend most of his day lying on a bed, in a front room where he could observe his beloved apple orchard, and watch for anyone who might come to call.

At four years old I would enter the room and, at my mom's urging, walk nervously toward this man whose hands and head shook uncontrollably. When he heard my slow approach, he would rise up on one forearm, wave his other hand at me and say in a still firm voice, "Come see me my damn little Democrat," and smile with a toothless grin when I ran to his bedside.

He was caring—As a young girl, my mom contracted chicken pox and became so ill the family doctor had given little Polly up for lost. The physician told Lester and Alice that little could be done for their girl. The youngest daughter couldn't eat and was getting weaker each day. Lester didn't accept that prognosis; he searched to find nourishment and discovered that his daughter could swallow warm milk. Gramps would rise every hour and milk a cow so Pauline could receive nourishment. Eventually my mom regained her health, married and raised three robust boys who went on to have families of their own.

He wasn't necessarily a good businessman—While Lester had a large farm and earned enough to take care of his family, it's been said that "he would spend $20 dollars to drive the 15 miles to Waterville to sell a $10 pig."

He loved the outdoors—Lester was an avid trout fisherman and hunter. And, in an effort to keep his family fed there are more than one incident where he had a brush with the local game wardens. One of the family's favorite stories is the night that Gramps decided to harvest some fresh meat that had been feeding on the cash crop in his nearby orchard.

The incident occurred one crisp

November night and the air grew colder by the minute. A black cloud blinded the bright harvest moon creating a night that was darker than a pocket. The Farmers' Almanac predicted a hard frost, the perfect weather for deer to move and to feed.

Lester climbed up onto the limb of one of his favorite Macintosh trees. Under the cover of night, he perched on a board; jammed bench-like between two extended tree limbs. Once settled, he rested his feet on a lower plank that had also been positioned in the tree stand earlier that day in preparation for the night-time hunt.

The evening's excursion had begun about 9:30 P.M. when Gramps exited through a back kitchen door, into an ell—an extended wing of the house—that served as a woodshed and a covered walkway which connected the house to the barn.

Leaving the radiant warmth of the kitchen's Star Kineo cookstove, Lester deliberately entered the cold dim light of the dingy hallway and eased a canvas pack onto his back. He bent to picked up his 1893 Winchester 30-30 rifle with a flashlight already attached to the gun's octagon barrel. Once equipped he faded through a darken doorway into the November air. Gramps moved with purpose, careful to not display any interior lighting that would disclose someone had exited the house.

Dressed for an evening outside, the hunter slightly shivered as he marched to his post. When he arrived at the previously prepared tree, Gramps used the branches like a ladder and climbed until he was six feet off the ground. With the cloudless dark, came penetrating cold, but he was prepared. He'd used this tree before.

Lester spread a buffalo robe over his legs and beneath this furred robe he struck a match, careful to hide the flare. With the flame he lit a kerosene lantern and placed the lamp on the footrest between his rubber pacs. Gramps had learned years before that the oil burning lamp was the perfect heat source, sure to keep his legs and feet warm.

Family legend states that my grandfather sat quiet, unmoving for some time when he heard a loud snap. He snapped towards the sound, his eyes searched for an identifiable shape moving in the blackness. The noise that echoed loud against the cold curtain of dark had to be caused by an animal or something that had stepped on a frost-covered tree branch. Alert with every muscle ready, Lester watched for any movement, of any kind—the moon peeked from behind a cloud just long enough for my grandfather to recognize the silhouette of a man and see a glint of light that reflected off a bronze badge.

Gramps immediately doused the lantern, threw the buffalo robe aside and slid off the opposite side of the fruit tree and headed back to the house. As he ran, Lester heard the sound of footsteps in hot pursuit following behind. Being a big, but long-legged man on home ground, Lester quickly outdistanced his pursuer.

My grandfather slightly opened the shed door, and slid sideways inside where he strode through the pantry way. Once in the warm house, he quickly unloaded the deer gun, removed the flashlight, and placed the firearm at its sentinel post beside the wood box; just inside the back kitchen door.

Someone pounded on the front door of the farmhouse and demanded entry. Lester hung his hat and coat on a nearby coat tree, lowered his suspenders, removed his boots and took off his woolen shirt which he threw over the back a nearby kitchen chair. Semi-dressed Gramps opened the top three buttons of his year round-undergarment of white cotton long-johns. Unfastening the top button of his pants and messing his hair to appear that he had just risen, my grandfather took a deep breath, turned up the kerosene lamp on the kitchen table that served as the family's nighttime illumination, and answered the door.

Standing on the front stoop were two game wardens dressed in their blue wool garb, so he yawned and asked sleepily, "Can I help ya guys?"

The wardens officially questioned, "We are chasing someone who was night hunting in your orchard, up the hill a ways. You seen anyone?" they commanded.

"Lord no," Gramps replied and continued, "I've been in bed ever since dark. It's much too cold to be outside tonight. Good luck finding 'em though; and thanks for protecting my crops."

He then sent the wardens off with a, "Hope you catch him." Thus Gramps had escaped a brush with the law, so he closed the door and went to bed while the wardens peered throughout the night for their man.

Indeed—my grandfather had a reputation.

He was a storyteller, a respected farmer, a proud family man, and an individual who sometimes made mistakes; but he was also a person who sought only to love his family, keep them healthy, safe, and happy. Grandfather was someone who struggled to pay his bills, the same goals and challenges that all of us aspire to each and every day of our lives.

But what does my family really know about this man who lived on this earth for nearly ninety years and went to his maker in 1958 when I was nine? Then again, what do any of us really know about our heritage? And can it be argued that the story of each generation of the family unit is also the account of experiences that have shaped our lives?

In the pages to follow the reader will meet one such family, their trials, their hopes, and sometimes— their fears. How much do you know about your ancestors? How much do you want to know?

Lester Stevens after a fishing trip at his home on Hilton Hill.
Photograph by Lester's oldest daughter and Tim's aunt, educator and
author Elinor Stevens Walker.

PROLOGUE

A tall stranger strides confidently towards the gates of a cemetery in central Maine. He is alone, because today's visit is something that requires full concentration and one that cannot be shared. Once inside, the man paused to scan the gray waves of headstones that stand resilient in an ocean of green. While the visitor considers the task at hand he also values the weighty role of the granite memorials that pays tribute to those interred; men, women, and children who once walked the earth.

The man's skin is tanned deep brown, his chest broad, arms muscular. He is wearing a green trail cap, red checkered shirt, green cotton pants, and is clean shaven—the everyday attire of a Maine woodsman. He walks straight and proud; his posture a result of physical exercise received from years of working in the Maine outdoors. The visitor passes through the wrought iron gate where marble statuettes sit majestically on manicured grass and ornamental hardwoods shade visitors from summer's heat.

The lone man has come to pay his respects to someone he's never met—a grandfather— his Pépé—a relative who died before today's visitor was born. A first-time caller to this hallowed ground, the grandson had been surprised years before when he discovered a letter from this deceased relative. This message from the past was his only connection with a gramps he'd only heard about.

In the sanctuary the caller examines the monuments for any sign of his family name. After a few minutes of searching he finds a headstone that proudly displays the name of Clark. Locating his grandfather's memorial he stoops and with gentle hands, brushes away the green moss that has partially filled in the chiseled letters. Once clean he reads the inscription on the stone:

JAMES PAUL CLARK

BORN NOVEMBER 16, 1938

DIED JUNE 1, 1993

THE SPIRIT STILL LINGERS IN A

FOREST PLACE ...

Caressing the carved letters of his grandpa's name, the man feels the tingle of a slight electrical shock prickle through his body. Touching the cold tombstone, the woodsman considers all he's been told about this man he's never met.

As a child, the woodsman had been told that his Pépé had hunted, fished, and explored the four corners of the state. Although his grandpa had loved to roam the woods, his mom had said the grandfather's time had been consumed with raising a family and operating a business. Even so, there were those who said that he'd been a rugged man with a keen sense of humor and one who often wrote poetry. The grandson had also learned he was the spitting-image, in look and mannerisms, of his gramps.

Today's visitor mulls over the circumstances that have brought him to this point in his life; and he stands quietly for several minutes. Finally the caller crouches on his right knee, rests his left hand on the top of the stone and speaks to this granite representation of a man who seemed larger than life. "Hi Grampa, we've never met. My name is Jim and I read your letter."

Jim, with his right hand, then removes a narrow ribbon from around his neck. Hanging from the end of the necklace dangles a large 1838 Liberty penny. For a moment the visitor studies the slightly tarnished surface of the antique coin that still captures a portion of the sun's reflection. Jim briefly remembers the luck the currency represents, and then carefully drapes the medallion so it hangs like a medal over the marker. With his mission accomplished, Jim straightens and walks back to his vehicle. As he moves away the coin invisibly melts into the monument, perhaps in preparation for another assignment.

Reader's Notes:

INTRODUCTION
MANY YEARS LATER IN BANGOR, MAINE ...

A solitary woman peers through the window of her third-story apartment and stares at the river below. Though dressed in a thick wool sweater, insulated zumba pants, and wool slipper socks she shivers from the cold. The lady stood behind the windowpane that provides the room's only access to daylight and a view of the outside world; wintery temperatures penetrated the single pane glass. For a second, the female considered turning up the thermostat of her one-room rent, but then remembered this month's bill for fuel oil is past due; so the occupant cradles a mug of hot coffee with both hands and welcomes the warmth from the cup's radiant heat.

Her housing isn't expensive and some say the flat is rundown, but the room meets her needs, and the roof doesn't leak. She reminds herself that the rental is only temporary, and for now it is all a young reporter can afford on a meager salary. This is especially true now that the repayment demands of her college financing have kicked in. For the next several years she'll just have to make do with even less disposable income, until the loans are paid back. *Someday*, she promises, *someday, I'll have a bigger place with large, sunny, efficient windows and a furnace that provides consistent heat.*

A flicker in the sky draws her attention to the sun's reflection from the snowy head of an American bald eagle. Soaring high over the river, the bird of prey suddenly drops to the swirling waters below. The girl follows the raptor's movement and watches the bird snatch an Atlantic salmon out of the icy liquid. Holding its prize in a firm clutch, the bird flies to the opposite shore and lands on the dead limb of a tall pine. Once settled, the scavenger holds the salmon with the spur of one talon and opens and closes its beak, as if speaking in anger.

With the apartment's window closed, the woman can't hear the sounds the eagle is making, but she has heard them before. The previous summer the reporter had watched through the apartment's open window when America's symbol had flown to the top of a nearby hemlock with its fresh catch. There, holding the salmon secure in sharp talons, the lady heard the bird's multi-noted scream as the bird bragged about capturing such a tasty meal.

Thinking of lunch made the lady's stomach growl and she remembered that her cupboard was bare and the refrigerator almost empty. Hungry, the girl's mouth watered at the thought of broiling a mess of fresh caught salmon.

Today her view is of the mighty Penobscot River, a waterway that surges and churns with heavy flows, but it's to the river's headwaters where her thoughts turn. The Penobscot is a watercourse of history, a place where ancients, Indians, loggers, and aquatic wildlife have lived and sought sustenance for years. A lifeblood of water that is amassed from thousands of acres of woodlands,–where liquid corpuscles become brooks, streams, and tributaries, which grow into life-sustaining arteries to pulse with energy from the heart of the Maine's forest, eventually growing into a torrent of water on its way to the salty Atlantic. In the past few months, the reporter had learned that one of the major vessels that feeds the Penobscot, is the carotid river called the Allagash, a multi-stemmed artery that delivers life-giving water from the state's headwaters to the body of Maine.

It's amazing what's gone on in them thar woods the lady smiled as she recalled the downeast drawl of her friend and remembered the task at hand. She left the window behind and took a seat at the kitchen table. There she stared at the manuscript waiting on the screen of her laptop.

For weeks the reporter had been consumed by an assignment. The interview wasn't a task she wanted, and a story she tried to refuse. But the paper's editor had held his resolve and ordered her to write the piece for the paper.

Entering the toil reluctantly, the lady soon became devoted to the fulfillment of the report and she'd learned—*oh how she has learned*! About noon the story was finally finished, so the woman spent the rest of the afternoon proofreading, correcting, editing, and polishing her first major project for which she would be paid.

At six o'clock that night she concluded that the day was done and so was the exposé. The lady walked to the cupboard and pulled out her only bottle of cabernet sauvignon; a housewarming treat provided weeks before by a former roommate and her only friend.

Sitting back down at the work station, aka dinner table, the reporter clicked the **ABC** spelling and grammar icon to make *this time the really* final review of the text. When the symbol on screen confirmed "Spelling and grammar check complete with no edits necessary," she checked the ok button, and hit *send*. Once the document was launched she closed the lid of her laptop. In a flash the story was electronically delivered to the receiving computer in the office of the editor for the Penobscot Basin Times, no longer *just hers* but an account to be shared with the world.

Leaning back in her chair, she took a gentle sip of the celebratory wine and reflected about the completed project. Months before the paper's editor had assigned her to interview a well-respected, elderly resident from the little town of Millinocket. "The man," the editor had said, "was at one time a park ranger esteemed for his dedication to duty and outdoor skills." Now *put out to pasture* the aged woodsman resided in a retirement community in Bangor. Doctors expected the geezer would spend his remaining days at the hospice, quietly growing older until called to his spiritual home.

It seemed like eons had passed when the fresh-out-of-college graduate, had been summoned to the city desk of the editor-in-chief. Only on the job for five days, the probationary employee worried that she had done something wrong as she walked nervously down the narrow aisle towards the boss's office. The dark brown carpet, laid like a well-traveled path, silently marked the way past a multitude of gray cubicles. From the open doorway of each workstation came the subtle clacking sound of correspondents that pounded away on electronic keyboards; in an effort to have their 'extra' ready for the evening edition. Not one of her co-workers noticed the passage of the new employee.

At the end of the corridor Margaret stood at the entrance of the solid glass enclosure. Centered onto the surface of the door window had been painted gold embossed lettering that confirmed the importance of the person inside. She knocked on the door's frame just to the left of

MARKUS FRASER, EDITOR
PENOBSCOT BASIN TIMES

and waited.

Positioned so the chief could monitor the activity throughout the news room; the man toiled behind a solid oak antique desk. Without lifting his head, the room's occupant raised his eyes, peered over the black rim of his framed bifocals and considered the individual who requested entry. Recognizing the new hire, he hollered, "Come in!" Entering a work space best described as cluttered; Margaret noticed the area around the desk was fortified by boxes of day-old circulations, heaps of advertisements and piles of books. On walnut paneled walls behind the desk; hung achievement plaques as testimonials to the reporter turned editor. One inscription acknowledged Mr. Fraser as "Newsman of the year" and another as the "Best New England Journalist of the decade." Nearby on grey file cabinets sat a variety of brass literary trophies–coated with dust.

On the wall closest to the framed desk were a collection of personal pictures. Two stood out above the rest. The first, the cub reporter noted, was of a young Mark Fraser, overweight and puffy. The man was standing with others on a campsite-all holding lit cigarettes while they admired a catch of squaretails laid out on the seat plank of a picnic table. In the first picture behind the men, exposed on the table's eating surface was a scattered array of empty beer cans, whiskey bottles and cigar wrappers.

The second photograph, more recent, portrayed a different view of her boss; this snapshot presented an older editor with slightly gray hair, but considerable thinner who had the sculptured features of someone who exercised daily. The editor posed, grinning, beside a man in uniform while a golden retriever sat between the two. Alert, the dog stared at the cameraman in an effort to determine if the shutterbug happened to carry any dog biscuits.

Timidly standing in place, the young reporter waited for her boss to break the silence. After five uncomfortable minutes positioned in front of a desk littered with a phone, two computers, an electronic tablet, calculator and scattered yellow post-em notes; the publishing supervisor instructed her to 'take a chair.' Once his newest hire was seated; the editor leaned back in his swivel chair and explained that he wanted her to do *the more than likely* 'old man's' final interview; and this was an assignment he *must insist* "be completed."

"The ranger, is an old friend," the editor had explained, "who is approaching his 85th birthday, and is someone who once saved my life." Continuing, the editor told how the incident occurred one spring; when the publishing supervisor had been a young reporter that struggled to build a career. 14 hour days and seven day work weeks had caused the young man to turn to doughnuts, coffee, cigarettes and too many hours sitting at a desk; where he grappled with deadlines. Finally his friends had talked him into taking a vacation into the Maine woods. It was there the editor had met a young ranger and received a once in a lifetime opportunity to reshape his life.

"In good conscious," the publishing supervisor insisted, "the paper can't let the old garde du parc, fade into oblivion without one last thank you from the public for whom the woodsman had served so well for so many years." With that, the editor's phone had rung and with a turn of his head and a wave of his hand; she'd been dismissed.

*****

Today the cub reporter remembered that the first meeting with former Ranger James Paul Clark hadn't gone very well. In fact their meeting had been so awkward she'd almost quit the paper. But needing the income the job provided the woman had gone back for another try and eventually discovered a door to another world, a natural realm that she'd only heard about but never visited. The more the reporter and ranger talked, the more cerebral cobwebs had been swept from his mind; once forgotten memories were recalled and translated into a mental treasure trove of outdoor adventures. The weekly visits flew by and after three months the cub reporter had finished a story she believed to be like no other.

But now her job was done and she prayed that someone out there in the cyber world of *reporting it like it is* would find her labors worthwhile.

But reporter Margaret Woodward wasn't sure, *no-sir-ree* she wasn't sure at all.

Within two days Editor Fraser announced the release of Margaret's efforts.

PENOBSCOT BASIN TIMES
Penobscotbasintimes.com

OUR MAINE MAN
By MARK FRASER
PBT Editor

A psychological study of any man from Maine will reveal that he is a complex creature, a person whom at any given time will display an "alpha to omega" gamut of personality traits. Such behavior is one that is immediately recognized by anyone *from away* as distinctly downeast.

Our fellow is intelligent and yet reckless. He is disarrayed but cautious. He listens to country music and takes his family to the opera. He and his wife enjoy the music of classic rock and roll; then he drives his daughter to the ballet.

Our guy cherishes books about the American West, the Revolutionary and Civil War, but enjoys poetry by lyricists such as New England's Robert Frost and Scotland's Robert Burns.

He's at home in the deep woods and can find his way without the compass that is always tucked in his left shirt pocket. But in the city, he'll curse the traffic and drive the wrong way down a one-way street in the Old Port, so *the Missus* can probe the rows of tourist traps on Portland's Commercial Street.

One moment he is cheered by his peers for his independence and cursed the next because he won't *just go along.* When shopping, this man will dicker all day to get a cheaper price and yet pay double the asking price for a box of Girl-Scout cookies.

He'll complain about the *flatlanders* being in the way but speak with pride about tracing his family roots to the pilgrims of Plymouth Colony in Massachusetts.

He'll hold his head high and support his family, but silently wonder why he can't do more on such a meager income. Our man will toil day and night to earn enough to get by, but he'll secretly leave food on the doorstop of a neighbor who has experienced hard times.

This man curses politics and the decisions the government makes; yet he will go to war at a moment's notice to fight for his country. He attends the basketball games at the local school, and quietly sheds a small tear when the flag is raised and the national anthem played. The ceremony reminds him of the time when he too played sports and represented his family and community.

While this person is loved, he is also hated; he is respected, and he is detested. He is cheered and yet ostracized. Some days he doesn't want to go to work, but he does, knowing that the weekend will bring time to spend with family and friends. Yes, he is a complicated machine—the person who lives in this place—we proudly call home. His is an individuality found in every man, woman, boy, and girl of our state; for he is one of us, and we are a part of him, this man of Maine.

In the next few weeks the Penobscot Basin Times is proud to offer a series of weekly interviews by reporter Margaret Woodward. This dialogue charts the exploits of one such native, retired Ranger James Paul Clark; welcome aboard while we voyage along on this man's sea of life.

Reader's Notes:

1
"IT'S MARGARET—IF YOU DON'T MIND!"

"Daddy, I missed you when you went to Allagash Lake!" the little girl excitedly announced when he walked in the front door of their house, tickled to death that her father was home. Just as the dad reached to give his daughter a hug; the child's voice faded and the man felt a hand on his shoulder and heard an adult voice command "Mister Clark, Mister Clark! Wake up, Mister Clark, there is someone here to see you!" the nurse declared and as she jiggled the right shoulder of the old man dozing in a rocking chair.

Awakened from his afternoon nap, the LPN caregiver had brought the resident back to a startling consciousness, ending the man's favorite image. The musing was a daydream the elder had often and was one he enjoyed. In his prime almost 65 years ago, the old man had worked as a ranger assigned to the Allagash corridor of the Maine woods. During the summer his family would share the space of a three-room ranger's cabin on Allagash Lake. However during the school year his wife, two sons and a four-year-old-daughter would move back to their modest home in Millinocket so the kids could get an education.

Back then, the ranger's work schedule required that the man remain at the job site eleven days and then be allowed three days off. Every eleventh day, at the end of the last hour of his shift, anxious and lonely for his wife and children, he'd drive a four-wheel drive truck over dusty gravel roads, and if he didn't get a flat tire or run into a moose; the family man could be home in three to four hours. Whenever he arrived in the yard of their modular home, the father would see the grinning face of his daughter Isabella, or Bella, as he called her, watching through the glass window of the door, impatiently waiting for her dad.

Once the little girl saw her father's tan pickup enter the driveway, she would jump up and down with excitement and loudly announce to their golden retriever "Daddy's home, Daddy's home!" With the dog barking a canine greeting, the child would climb onto the seat of the nearest chair and wait for her father to come inside. As soon as he opened the door the girl would jump through the air confident she'd be caught by her father's strong arms and exclaimed, "Daddy, I missed you when you went to Allagash Lake."

Snapped out of his afternoon snooze, the old man looked up at the nurse and saw a woman standing beside the caregiver. Reaching out a tanned right hand, the lady introduced herself, "Hi Mr. Clark, my name is Margaret Woodward and I am a reporter for the Penobscot Basin Times and I'd like to interview you." The nurse, realizing that introductions were complete, turned to deliver an afternoon dose of medicine to the patient in room five.

"Why is that?" the old man said suspiciously, unsure why he'd been woken and yet curious about the stranger standing before him.

"I cover the outdoors for the paper and I understand that you were a ranger for a number of years.

Rising slowly to give what appeared to be a stiff back time to straighten, the gentlemen stood in front of his chair and stuck out a huge, shaky, right hand, smiled and said, "Hi, Maggie, guess that'd be ok, but only if you call me Jim." She extended her hand to complete their greeting and replied "Ok Jim but" then she reminded the old man, "but my name is Margaret."

Nodding he thought, *Independent lady I guess, but that's ok* and then replied, "I was a ranger for a while, spent some time in the woods, suppose there may be a couple of experiences you'd be interested in."

Appraising his visitor, Jim thought her young, maybe in her early to mid-20's, and dressed to be comfortable. An open L.L. Bean coat, a Baxter State parka, exposed the reporter's selection for today's wear. The elder saw that the woman was outfitted with a red wool sweater, green bush pants, and wearing classic L.L. Bean boots. Carrying a matching waterproof day pack looped over one shoulder, the girl was ready for a walk to the office or a stroll through the forest. *Fashionable, but probably inexperienced*, Jim speculated. *All her garb appears to be brand-new store bought. Wonder if she can handle herself in the woods or if she dressed for show? Too bad she forgot to remove the price tag still hooked to the zipper tab of the pack.*

Jim estimated his visitor to be about five feet

four or five inches tall with a strong medium size frame that appeared accustomed to exercise. The caller had an hourglass figure that, in his younger days, would have caught Jim's attention no matter where he was. Long brown hair speckled with streaks of blond, bleached by the sun, flowed onto her shoulders. In her left hand she carried an electronic tablet, *to take notes for the story I guess,* thought Jim. The grip of her right hand was strong, like she was comfortable carrying her own gear. *Pretty girl–a little thin–but pretty. I bet she doesn't weigh 110 pounds soaking wet.* But still there was something that made the former woodsman question if she was original or simulated; *or if she could possibly be the one he's been waiting for?*

Reader's Notes:

2
THE ASSIGNMENT

I hate these mundane interviews the cub reporter thought as she drove from the parking lot of the Penobscot Basin Times and headed toward the Pleasant Ridge Assisted Living Community and her latest assignment. Margaret had been at the paper for only a short time, and she had accepted the job to be an outdoor reporter in order to *be outdoors–not doing human interest interviews with folks living in wrinkle city.* That's why she'd used the last of this month's paycheck to buy the new outfit to wear in the forest, not sitting at a desk.

Arriving at The Community, Margaret found an empty parking space beside a brown 4x4 GMC pickup. Locking the door of her third-hand car, the visitor walked by the truck and noticed that the vehicle was blanketed by dust and the truck's right front tire was flat. Thinking that the *pickup hasn't been moved in a while,* Margaret continued toward a building constructed to appear friendly, yet the illuminated numbered security pad beside a soundproof, locked, plate glass door stated otherwise.

The reporter sighed with reluctance and pushed the buzzer to notify the attendant that someone wanted entry. "May I help you?" a receptionist's cheery voice asked over the crackling clamor that emitted from a nearby speaker.

Gazing through the glass entrance, Margaret saw a woman sitting behind an imitation wooden desk laden with vases of flowers, a personal computer, and a rose-colored telephone. Margaret answered, "I am a reporter with the Penobscot Basin Times and I am here to interview a Mr. Clark."

"Oh yes, your editor called. We've been expecting you."

The static sound of a buzzer followed by a loud click announced that the door was now unlocked and she was permitted in. Walking to the greeter's desk, the reporter was instructed, "Please sign in and I'll provide an identification tag for you to wear. Would you like a cup of coffee?"

"No thanks, I just had an energy drink. Where will I find Mr. Clark?"

"He's always in the day-room this time of day

watching the bird feeders on the back porch." The receptionist then pointed the way toward a nearby room from which the refrain of a soap opera boomed from the surround sound of a 52-inch TV. "The nurse will show you the way."

"Why was the door locked?" the reporter asked. "Are you expecting trouble?"

"Oh no," the receptionist answered. "It's just that a few of our family suffer from dementia and every once in a while, in confusion, they'll try to walk away. We keep the entrance locked for their safety."

Placing the looped nylon cord of the identification tag around her neck, Margaret nodded that she understood and followed a woman wearing light green scrubs, a fashion favored by health-care workers. Entering an intersection where two hallways crossed, Margaret paused briefly and looked up and down the corridors. As far as she could see there were apartment doors staggered along each wall and labeled with names and a variety of decorations. The adornments on each door identified the family name and hinted at the interests of the occupants inside.

Entering the dayroom, Margaret saw a host of four-wheel rolling walkers lined up in parallel parking fashion, waiting patiently for their drivers to take 'em for a spin. The nurse and visitor entered the well-appointed room. Sprinkled about the area were groups of senior citizens engaged in a variety of activities. People were playing cards, games of scrabble, and reading; while others watched TV, intently focused on the passionate daytime drama "As the Seasons Fall." From the television, Margaret could hear yet another pretty starlet ask her *too* handsome boyfriend "if he was sure she was the only one?"

Still others in the sunny room were enjoying an afternoon nap, snoozing; unmindful of everyone and everything.

Those still awake looked up when Margaret appeared. Each one of the residents attempted eye contact with the pretty new arrival in order to grasp any opportunity to visit with somebody new, some even offered the greeting of "hello dear." But Margaret followed closely behind her LPN guide and ignored the obvious overtures from those she passed.

Paying little attention to the television, the nurse stopped to help a resident in a wheelchair pick up a book written by a Maine author titled *Headin' North,* a paperback that had slipped from a weak hand onto the floor. This pause gave Margaret the opportunity to stare at the back of the head of a lone man in a rocking chair on the other side of the room, sitting directly in front of the glass of a sliding double door. Outside flocks of birds were viciously attacking suet, sunflower, and thistle seeds stored in well stocked feeders.

Margaret didn't know why she had focused on him, but something indicated this man was different from the others. Snoring softly, the man was obviously asleep, but still there was something, something she felt rather than saw and that sensation—like a magnet—drew her gaze towards him.

Dressed in a woodsman's attire of a checkered red and black light wool shirt, green work pants, wool stockings and moccasins the reporter thought *he's dressed rather odd for being inside–it's so warm in here. It's like he is waiting to leave. Maybe he is one of the people that the receptionist told me about and the reason that the door is locked? Great, just the type of interview that will help my career—NOT!*

Appraising her assignment Margaret noticed that despite his obvious age he still had a full head of brown hair with just a fringe of silver. The man's skin carried a permanent tan pigmented from working years in the sun. Jim's hands were large and callous from days of man-handling axes, chainsaws, and canoes. When he opened his eyes and stood in respect of the nurse's introduction, the reporter saw that the man was of larger than medium build and behind the fellow's bifocals his hazel eyes were clear and burned with intelligence. At six feet, Jim towered over the two women standing in front of him.

"I'd like to do an interview, and I've got all day," the reporter quickly stated as if she had nothing else to do, and then asked, "Where's the best place to talk?"

"Right here is ok, I suppose. You can pull a chair up from the table along the far wall," Jim said and pointed to the other side of the room. Sliding the seat close to Mr. Clark's rocking chair, Margaret opened her iPad while Jim reassumed a position of comfort in his favorite chair. Unsure and feeling like she was walking across unfamiliar ground, Margaret began with her first question, "So you spent time in the woods. Did you like it?"

Jim answered, "Yes."

Expecting more of a response Margaret electronically typed his answer and continued, "Did you stay there long?"

"Yes," was Mr. Clark's only offer.

Sensing the interview wasn't off to a very good start Margaret cleared her throat and probed further,

"Did you ever get lonely?"

"No," was the only answer.

Exasperated Margaret put down her tablet and said, "Mr. Clark, you aren't helping me much. Can you please try and reply with complete sentences?"

"Suppose I could, but let me ask you a few questions first."

"Well, ok, I guess," Margaret reluctantly replied.

"Have you ever hunkered down, Miss Woodward?"

"**Excuse me!** Hunkered down? I'm not sure what you mean." The lady reporter suddenly felt intimidated by such an unusual question.

"Have you ever had an outboard motor cavitate?"

"Not that I know of," she said, unsure of what cavitate even meant.

"Ever traipsed a snowshoe trail into a deer yard on the coldest day of winter only to find a slightly warmer forest? A place that provides relief against the cold so you decide to cut down a small cedar so starving whitetails could feed on its branches?"

Not waiting for her answer Jim continued to interrogate, "Have you ever been in the north Maine woods at all, Miss Woodward?"

"No, "Margaret said blushing and suddenly not feeling very good about this assignment, not at all!

"Well, I tell you what. We'll do an interview but first let's set a few ground rules, shall we?"

Taken by complete surprise with Mr. Clark's aggressive approach, she only nodded in the affirmative, so he continued, "Here's what you do: first study a map of the north woods. When I talk about Johnson Pond, I am going to expect that you'll be able to show me where the pond is on a map, how far it is from Millinocket, and tell me how to get there.

"Second, pick up books to read about the Allagash woods—that part won't be hard—dozens have been written. I recommend at least three, *The Allagash* by Legendary Maine Guide Gil Gilpatrick, *The Wilderness from Chamberlain Farm* by Dr. Dean Bennett, and lastly, *Solace* by former Ranger Supervisor Tim Caverly. You'll find a lot of solid information in those volumes.

"Finally, think about the information you want and the questions you need to ask. When you come back, if you do return, bring at least 10 well-thought-out questions that are not open-ended. If you want a good story, then you'll need to stimulate this old memory. Good day, Miss Woodward." Dismissing the reporter, Jim settled back into his rocking chair, leaned his head against the headrest and closed his eyes.

Stunned Margaret stared briefly at the man— she then closed her tablet, stood up, grabbed her coat from the back of her chair and mumbled to herself as she turned to leave–*I've never been talked to in such a manner. In my college writing class I composed some good papers and always got A's! Who does this old man think he is talking to? Why I've got a good mind...* when she neared the hallway he shouted "Maggie!"

She turned to look back at this man who still sat with his eyes closed and heard him instruct, "Come back next Monday at 7 A.M., I work best in the morning. Plan on having tea and tell my good friend, your editor Mark, that I said hi."

Feeling so mad she could *just spit nails* Margaret stomped out of the room as the old gent called out one last command, "And don't walk by my neighbors without smiling and saying hi either."

Furious, the only retort the reporter for the Penobscot Basin Times could formulate was to shout over her shoulder, "**The name is Margaret!**" With that the lady threw her identification onto a magazine table, stormed through the reception area, and slammed the glass door shut behind her.

In a distant corner of the cheery room sat a man nestled deep in an overstuffed recliner. Grizzled with a furrowed brow, wrinkled cheeks and parched lips, the fellow's face read like a roadmap of experience. The man's presence was in direct contrast to the warmness of the surroundings. Situated in such a way to be unnoticed, and yet still monitor the room, he saw everyone who entered or left.

Years before the gentleman had been tall but now was bowed and bent. His hair had turned from coal black to a thinning powdery gray. Jutting beyond the cuffs of his wool shirt were large hands, inflamed and swollen with arthritis. So sore, the appendages appeared an angry red against the backdrop of the man's green plaid top. Fingers, once strong and true, now trembled uncontrollably, and protested against any task; even the simple chore of holding the pages of the daily news.

His hands were only a part of a body that for years had been exposed to nature's elements. A physique that now bared the signs of abuse from days of lying excessively beside too many winter ice fishing holes where, in subzero conditions, he scooped out the slush with bare hands; too absorbed by a nibbling brook trout to slip on gloves.

Today unobserved and with knowing eyes, the old timer scrutinized a scene he'd watched a dozen times. Once satisfied his friend was ok; the old man returned to study the editorial section of the Penobscot Basin Times and muttered, "Good luck little girl."

Reader's Notes:

3
RETURNED

Seven days later at 6:45 A.M., Margaret drove into the parking lot of the Pleasant Ridge Community. She parked beside the same dusty pickup, locked her car, and walked to the main entrance. At the door she paused, took a deep breath, exhaled slowly and pushed the intercom call button for permission to enter.

Recognizing the reporter, the receptionist smiled, handed Margaret an identification badge, and pointed at Mr. Clark, sitting in his rocking chair with his back to the receptionist's cubical. The old man stared at the song birds on the home's back porch seemingly oblivious to Margaret's arrival. The greeter confirmed "He is waiting for you in the lounge."

Prepared to confront her assignment, Margaret walked directly to and around the back of the red rocking chair and stared at the face of Jim Clark.

Without rising he looked up to meet her stormy gaze as she stated, "Mr. Clark, I'll have you know that for the last week I've been hunkered down in the city's reading library. An outboard motor cavitates when the propeller turns in shallow water so that the blades creates a vacuum, and spins in a pocket of air instead of water. Unable to 'grab a hold' of the river; the engine loses torque.

"In order to reach Johnson Pond, I'll begin the three-hour trip by taking the Baxter Park Road out of Millinocket ten miles to the dike between Millinocket and Ambajejus Lakes. Across the street from the popular North Woods Trading post, the last stop for gas, gear and supplies but the best stop for food, drink and souvenirs." she quoted from the store's website and continued. "First I'll fill up with gas and grab lunch, and then turn left onto the Golden Road. After 20 miles or so, I'll take a right turn onto the gravel Telos Road, and follow the gravel highway until I reach the corner that lies just west of Chamberlain Bridge. At that sharp crook in the road, I'll turn left onto the Longley Stream Road, and continue north until the left turn at the Ledge Road in T7R14.

The junction road will deliver me to the north shore of Round Pond where I'll turn right onto the

Johnson Pond Road. After three hours I'll arrive at the parking lot and the path to the put-in at Johnson Pond. From that access a person can canoe across the pond to Johnson Stream and down the small watercourse until they reach upper Allagash Stream, then it's downstream with the current into Allagash Lake.

"A whitetail deer eats white cedar in the winter because grass isn't available. The coniferous softwood contains the nutrition that the game animal needs in order to survive our extreme Maine winters. In the fall deer will grow hollow hair which provides insulation for heat, and the herd makes a network of trails through their yards in order to conserve energy. And at the first sign of heavy snow they will move to their protective cover–a winter yard.

"During the cold season, the deer yard is warmer than the surrounding area because the area has a southeast exposure, which is protected by the overhead canopy. Located in such a way, their wintertime pasture provides a shelter from the wind and one that is warmed by the sun. This same conifer shelter reduces snow depth so whitetails can live closer to the animals' comfortable depth limit of 18 inches, and thus browse easier. And furthermore, no I've never been to the north woods, but I am going there next summer."

Mr. Clark returned her stare and, for what seemed an eternity… neither spoke, but just glared at each other. Outside the sparrow-sized downy woodpecker nibbled at suet; while a host of song birds flittered about at feeders. A quick census would record that a black-masked cedar waxwing, the friendly black-capped chickadee, the tufted titmouse, and dark-eyed juncos clustered about; each one seeking the perfect spot to dine. Under each feeding station a mourning dove *coo-ah coo, cooed* a soft hello while a near-by temperamental red squirrel scolded and ordered the others to leave his food alone. But neither Miss Woodward nor Mr. Clark heard the commotion going on outdoors.

Jim slowly stood, allowed his gaze to meet the lady's until he turned to look at the birds. Once on his feet he pointed at the feeders and said, "It's a shame really. I like all the birds but my favorite is the gray jay. Legend says that the ashen-colored birds carry the spirit of dead lumberjacks and thus are never to be harmed. Never found far away from the deep woods, the white-face, black-billed little birds are also called Whiskey John, Camp Robber, or Gorby. One winter when I was surveying, I had two jays that were so curious; the birdies would fly into my cabin and land on the table and stand next to my plate and beg for food."

Margaret had almost decided that the old guy had finally lost it and was ready to leave when he stuck his hand out and said, "Good Morning Margaret, it is good to see you." Then Jim invited, "Have you eaten? I hope not because I asked the cook to make us breakfast. It's on the table waiting, come on, I'm starved."

Margaret didn't admit it, but she hadn't eaten since yesterday and so after returning his handshake she followed Mr. Clark with relish, feeling very relieved.

Between bites of bacon, eggs, home toast and swallows of coffee, Jim said, "I suspect the editor may have told you a little about me, but I don't know anything about you. How about telling me about yourself?"

"Well, there's not really much to share," the young lady began. "I am from a small town outside of Skowhegan and my history is typical of someone from a rural community. I graduated from high school and thanks to the encouragement of a teacher; I attended the University of Maine at Orono where I received a degree in Journalism with minors in Forestry and Biology.

"A few months ago I landed my first job; as a reporter for the Basin Times and that is why I am here."

"Why did you take the variety of studies?"

"Well I like to write, but I've also had some distant relatives who worked as fire wardens, game wardens. and rangers. I grew up hearing their stories and so I've always had an interest in the outdoors. I love to hunt, fish, and hike, but I've been so busy paying bills that there hasn't been much opportunity for me to explore Maine. I thought being an outdoor reporter would allow me to write about the natural world."

"Do you have brothers and sisters?

"No, I am an only child."

"How 'bout your folks?"

"They both died when I was young and I've been on my own ever since."

"Boyfriend?"

"No-I don't have time to date. But enough about me, let's get back to you." Margaret felt that Mr. Clark was getting a little too close to opening a door to memories that she didn't want to revisit right now. And this was a good time as any to change the subject.

"Please, call me Jim." The gentleman had been listening and watching his guest during the early morning meal. The way she wolfed down food, he suspected that despite wearing new duds, she was hungry and hadn't spent much money for food. He also noticed the cloud that veiled her eyes when he mentioned family. Jim was positive there was more to learn about this pretty and very thin young lady.

Reader's Notes:

4
THE EARLY YEARS

"When and where was the first time you ever went into the woods?" Margaret asked and begun the interview in earnest, "and why did you go?"

"I was about five years old and knee-high-to-a-grasshopper. My family lived in Cornville at the time." Jim answered and when he saw the puzzled look on Miss Woodward face, he continued. "I grew up on a small family farm and had a pet collie named Solo. Whenever my mom would scold me for getting too dirty or something else I'd done, I would cry and call to my dog. Off Solo and I would go into the woodlot behind our colonial home. There we'd find deer, partridge, songbirds, and rabbit in abundance. I never ventured very far and soon my collie and I had forgot about my mom's anger. We would become Davy Crockett and his trusted companion, protecting the woman folk of the settlement against attack. The Maine woods has been my sanctuary ever since."

"Were there other instances when you ventured into the forest as a young man?"

"Yes. For a few years I had a great uncle who worked as a ranger in Baxter State Park. So I spent many summers hiking around and over mile-high Mount Katahdin. One summer he was stationed at Russell Pond, a seven-mile hike into the interior of the sanctuary. I had a canoe and my fly rod and a good supply of an artificial flys called the White Miller. The Miller was my favorite for catching brook trout.

"At the remote campground there was also a tame deer that my uncle called Grandma. Grandma loved saltine crackers. So each night; just before dark, I would sit along the trail, some distance from the camp, and give her a treat. One day I was perched on a small rock feeding the doe saltines when all of a sudden she stamped both feet, snorted and somersaulted backwards into the forest. I couldn't imagine what had spooked the gentle creature.

"I remained motionless beside the woods path, unmoving until I heard a branch crack, an indication that the whitetail was moving. I watched and soon Grandma peeked under a fir branch and looked up and down the pathway. When she didn't see any danger, the whitetail stepped toward me and following close behind was a white-spotted brown fawn. The baby couldn't have been much more than a few days old. The doe had gone back to get her little one to show me. I offered Bambi a saltine, although he was too small to chew, he did lick the salty surface of the cracker. That was the closest I ever got to a newborn whitetail.

"Spending summers in Baxter must have been a lot of fun. Did you ever go into the park in the winter?"

"About every school vacation that I could. At every chance I'd hitch a ride to Millinocket to stay with my uncle, during one wintery visit I got a heck of a scare, though!"

"How's that?" Margaret felt encouraged now that her subject was speaking freely.

"It was February school vacation and I had just gotten my driver's license. At the time Baxter Park had an old Willy jeep that needed to be driven to town for repairs. About six o'clock one evening, on a night darker than a pocket, my uncle asked if I could drive the jeep and follow behind the park pickup. Of course I jumped at the opportunity and when I got behind the wheel he cautioned, 'Now remember Jim the roads are snow covered so don't follow too close and don't drive too fast.'

"Grinning, I couldn't wait to get going so I nodded in understanding. Well the trip went pretty well until about a mile north of the dike between Millinocket and Ambejejus Lakes. All of a sudden the truck my uncle was driving careened off the road into the ditch. His pickup hit the snow bank so hard that a white flurry flew through the air, over the park truck and covered the windshield of the little jeep.

"Immediately I jammed on my brakes and slid to a halt. I jumped out of the Willy's and ran to my uncle's vehicle just as he opened the door. Visibly shaken he uttered, 'I think I've killed someone!' Then he followed with, 'I've run over a snow sled. We've gotta find the body!' I looked at the front of his truck and saw that the vehicle's right front tire had come to a stop on top of a crushed cowling of an overturned yellow snowmobile.

"As you can imagine, at 16 years old the last thing I wanted to search for on a cold black evening was a dead person buried in the snow! Just as we grabbed a flashlight to search the ditches my uncle heard a hissing sound. He shouted, 'that's the air escaping from someone's lungs, oh my god!, he's under the truck!"

"We flashed our Maglites all about, but no-one could be seen. Then we saw a car coming and my uncle expecting the worst, exclaimed 'darn it! Here comes his wife and family!' But that wasn't the case, nope not at all."

By this time Margaret had become so interested in the story that she had stopped taking notes. Smiling, Jim reminded, "Did you wanna write this down?"

Slightly red faced at forgetting why she was there, Margaret replied, "Oh yes," and begun typing in earnest.

"Well the person in the vehicle happened to be a mechanic working at a small shop just up the road between the lakes at today's landmark the North Woods Trading Post. The service man explained that when he'd started a snowmobile to take it into the work area, the machine's throttle had frozen wide open. When the engine engaged, the clutch meshed in and ski-doo spun out of control–and threw the mechanic off.

"Eventually we figured out the machine had zigzag over a mile under its own power–without a headlight. The sled had bounced first off one snow bank only to careen off another, as the driverless snowmobile sped down the public way. And that was what my uncle had hit. Boy, it sure threw a scare into us and provided me with a lesson that I never forgot."

"And what lesson was that?"

Here Jim sat forward on the edge of the chair to emphasize that he firmly believed what he was about to say, "To pay attention, be prepared to handle anything that comes your way, and never–ever–panic!

"That lesson has served me very well and probably the reason I am still alive today."

"What do you mean?" Margaret asked.

Before Jim could answer a nurse interrupted the conversation by instructing the resident, "It's time to check your vital signs and for you to take your medicine, Jim. Please follow me to the infirmary."

The old man gave Margaret a look that said *here we go again*, turned to the nurse and said, "Nah– I'm fine. Go on and find someone else to poke."

"Now Mr. Clark," here Margaret heard firmness build in the nurse's voice as the caregiver questioned, "are you going to do as I say or do I need to call the orderly again?"

"Ah, don't make a fuss, I'll be a good boy,"

Jim said as he stood to follow the nurse. Winking at Margaret he said to the nurse, "I'll come along and won't argue. I don't have a lot of strength these days you know. Just let me say good-bye to my guest first."

Turning to the reporter Jim said, "A couple of years after the snowmobile incident I went to the University of Maine at Machias to earn a teaching degree. It was there, while in college, that I experienced the best thing that ever happened to me and also live through the worst thing possible."

Leaving Margaret behind, Jim followed turning his head to the right and while following the nurse, said over his shoulder, "Come on back in the morning, Maggie, same time and I'll tell ya about it."

Pleased with today's interview, the reporter watched the old man obediently follow the attendant so Margaret hollered a heartfelt "Thank you." Without turning, Jim held up his right arm and waved a firm hand to let Margaret know that he'd heard.

When Margaret started to walk toward the outside entrance, she noticed an elderly gray-haired old lady sitting at a small card table near the opening to the room. Intent on completing the puzzle, the old lady didn't see Margaret's approach. The resident was well dressed, wearing costume jewelry and sporting a fresh slightly blue colored hairdo. Holding a piece to the puzzle, she searched for a place to fit the jumble. Margaret stopped, studied the jigsaw for a minute and added a piece to the brainteaser. The woman looked up, smiled, and said "Thank you, dear." Margaret, feeling good, nodded "your welcome," and left the building on the way to her office to prewrite her report.

Reader's Notes:

5
THE BEST OF TIMES AND THE WORST OF TIMES

Rising early to allow for a few minutes of quiet and to enjoy her first cup of morning coffee, Margaret assumed her favorite perch in front of the window overlooking the river. Sipping the bitter brew, Margaret spied a flock of the colorful goldeneye ducks swimming below in the river's eddy. Locally the migratory birds were called whistlers due to the tune their wings made in flight. The web-footed hens and drakes bounced and bobbed in the foamy flow, at home along the edge of the swift current, searching for breakfast.

Watching the graceful waterfowl Margaret would have loved to eat breakfast too, but she just wasn't in the mood for any more of the ramen noodles that had become her daily fare. So she convinced herself that she wasn't really hungry and heartened, *and it's only five hours to lunch.*

Her day had started early so Margaret would have plenty of time to spare. But that schedule was suddenly spoiled when she tried to start the car. Planning to head off to work, Margaret turned the key in the vehicle's ignition but the only sound she heard was the click, click, click of the car's solenoid. A statement that announced the automobile had a dead battery.

Suddenly delayed because it took the Auto Club *sooo* long to show up and provide the necessary boost, the reporter was over an hour late when she pulled into her customary parking space beside the brown truck. Hurrying to make up for lost time, Margaret didn't notice that the flat tire on the four-wheel drive had been repaired.

Walking toward the front entrance, Margaret found the door unlocked and the office chair receptionist desk empty. So the reporter scribed her name on visitor line number 15 of the sign-in sheet and picked up the corresponding identification badge that waited beside the registration form. Thinking it odd that there wasn't an attendant by the front door, Margaret continued toward the dayroom.

Entering the hallway, Margaret heard the sound

of laughter echoing from down the corridor. Walking cautiously, so not to interrupt anyone's private party, she entered an auditorium full of people. Scanning the crowd, Margaret saw that every seat was taken and even attendants from the retirement village were standing about the walls. Every eye in the room was focused toward someone at the front of the room.

Following their gaze, Margaret was surprised to see Jim standing behind a podium, speaking.

"When I was young I had an Uncle Buzz who was a ranger in Baxter State Park and I often would spend summers with him. Well, one morning he and I were raking tent sites in the campground when several youngsters approached and one said, '*H*ey Ranger, can we ask ya something?' the apparent ringleader inquired.

" 'Sure,' "my Uncle Buzz answered as he eased down to take a seat on top of a nearby picnic table in order to give the early morning visitors his full attention.

'You live so far from town, how do you get fresh supplies?' "The leader of the half dozen boys and girls asked while the others gathered to listen. Feeling a little bored, the brood had walked down from their camping space in the Park's Abol

Campground, to find out what it was like to have a home in the woods.

" 'Living for the summer at the foot of Mt. Katahdin in Baxter State Park with my uncle, at eleven years old I wasn't much older than those posing the question. While the ranger prepared to answer the first question of the day, I remained quietly in the background; and listened. The adolescents kicked at stones along the edge of the roadway, eagerly awaiting his words.

" 'It's a long ways to the grocery store for sure, and we are very busy, so I really can't get away very often. We catch trout; pick native greens as best we can, have a small garden for those vegetables that we can't find in the woods, and as for milk, well, whenever we run out of milk . . .' and here my uncle placed a well-timed pause, rubbed his chin with one hand as if in deep thought, unsure if it was ok to share such a deep secret, exhaled with a deep sigh and answered, 'We milk a moose.'

"Every young mouth of his audience instantly dropped open and just as quick the kids shouted in unison, 'Wow! Milk a moose, really? Can we help? We've always wanted to milk a moose!'

"In no hurry to reply, my uncle took a minute,

scratched his head in cautious contemplation and said, 'Hmm . . . it's an unusual request, but I surrr-pose the female moose wouldn't mind.' Lowering his voice to almost a whisper to emphasize he was speaking in only the strictest confidence, 'I have trained the animal pretty well. But you have gotta be here early now; moose have a lot of ground to cover in a day, and the cow won't wait around very long.'

" 'Oh don't worry, we'll be here.' And with that the kids went skipping off toward the day's adventure of checking lean-tos and tent sites in search of any treasure that someone may have left behind.

"My uncle and I returned to our unglamorous tasks of raking campsites, cleaning outhouses, repairing picnic tables. Late that night, after a full day of chores and a midnight swim at Abol Beach, we dropped exhausted into bed.

"The next day, we arose at the crack of dawn and we walked down the creaking stairs to the pine smell of the rounded logs as the cabin invited us to a brand new day.

"It was my turn to make breakfast, so I placed the tea kettle to boil on the back of the wood cookstove for our first cup of hot ice-tea (this was at a time when neither of us drank coffee, and regular tea still tasted too bitter). I dug out the juice, milk, and fruit from the propane refrigerator, and just as we had begun to mix our hot beverage, he heard voices coming from the outside. Looking out the window pane of the cabin's office door, Uncle Buzz exclaimed, 'Oh my gosh! Here come the kids to help milk the moose!'

"Peering through the living room window I could see the group of six from the day before, skipping down the road from their campsite. heading toward our cabin. Excitedly the youths were singing, 'We're going to milk a moose, we're gonna milk a moose, hi-ho the dairy-o, we're gonna milk a moose!'

" 'What are we going to do?' "My Uncle spoke more to himself than to me. Before I could say *scat*, my uncle opened the kitchen cupboard, grabbed a box of Carnation Instant Milk and dumped the contents into a nearby empty galvanized bucket. He then added the hot water from the kettle simmering on the back of the stove to the dry mix. Grabbing a piece of cedar kindling from the wood box, he gave the mixture a quick stir, grabbed the pail, and flew out the back kitchen door, and hollered over his shoulder, 'You keep 'em busy.' As he headed out through the back door, there was a knock at the front door. I went out to say good morning to our young guests, and opened the door to the porch.

" 'We've come to help milk the moose,' they proudly announced like someone who had just discovered the cure for the common cold.

" 'Sorry, but you're too late. My uncle left about an hour ago and I don't know when he'll be back. I fibbed to the disappointed youths. Immediately their grinning faces melted into upside down smiles with an expressions so distressing I thought they were going to cry. Then from behind came the sound of music.

"The youths turned to see my uncle walking down the same road from where they had just come, carrying his warm bucket of instant milk. Moving easy he whistled a rendition of an old country song, *They call it that old mountain dew.*

"The group, moving as one, surrounded my uncle in the middle of the driveway and challenged, 'You've already milked the moose?'

"Stopping in mid-tune he replied sternly, 'I said you had to be here early, the moose left a few minutes ago to get her breakfast.'

" 'That's not moose milk!" a skeptical young fellow confidently stated as he did his best to hide his distress while he stared at the white foam in the bucket.

"While I continued to watch from the open door, the young Ranger offered, 'Try it.' The same disbelieving youth, stuck his trigger finger into the bucket and without hesitation licked his digit dry. With eyes wide, while the others waited impatiently for the verdict the youngster announced, 'By gosh! It is moose milk!'"

Here the whole room broke out into another round of laughter and Jim said, "Thanks for allowing me to share a story." The audience then broke out in an uproar of applause. Standing silently by the door, Margaret heard two residents say, "I just love Jim's stories!" "I hope he'll tell some more next week."

Walking gingerly up the center aisle as if walking on glass, Jim shook hands, and thanked people for coming. He didn't see Margaret until he neared the doorway. Sensing that someone was staring, the man and looked up, immediately smiled and said, "Why hello Maggie, I didn't know you were standing there."

"Sorry I'm late for our appointment," she said, not bothering to correct him.

"No worries," Jim said. "Today's scheduled

speaker canceled at the last moment so the activity director asked if I'd share some of my experiences to fill in. Did you like my story?"

Margaret responded, "Oh yes, I did. It was different than anything I'd ever heard before. Do you do this sort of thing often?"

"Oh now and then," Jim smiled and continued, "The folks here seem to like 'em."

"Is the *Milking the Moose* story true?"

"Mostly," Jim replied, "like I said, in my youth I spent many summers in Baxter Park. What I didn't know until years later was that my future wife was one of the kids in the group that wanted to do the milking. Let's go grab a coffee."

Walking side by side down the hall, Jim continued, "One summer I worked at Kidney Pond Sporting Camps in the park as a dishwasher. While the boys worked at Kidney, there were girls who worked at nearby York's Daicey Pond Camps. It was only a 20-minute walk through the forest. So at the end of our work day, two or three of us would head off. At first Jr. and Jeanette York, the owners of the Daicey camps welcomed us, but being teenage boys and the girls being cute; it didn't take long for us to wear out our welcome. One evening about dusk Mrs. York gathered us about and said, 'I don't want you Kidney Pond boys bothering my Daicey Pond girls, so go on back to Kidney where you belong.' Off we went back to our own camp, with head bowed. So much for us guys trying to carry on a backwoods romance."

Reaching the coffee bar in the dayroom Margaret saw that the lounge was once again crowded with residents carrying on a variety of activities, and smiled as she thought about Jim's stories. Pouring coffee, she asked, "Cream and sugar?"

"No thanks. I got tired of carrying milk and sugar in my canoe, so I learned to drink it black, but go ahead and grab some."

Stirring in a generous amount of sugar and cream in her cup, Margaret followed the man in the direction of his perch that overlooked the bird feeders. Close behind, the reporter watched Jim shuffle stiffly toward his favorite seat; and thought *my, he seems old and frail today.*

"During our previous conversation," Margaret asked as she took a seat to begin the interview, "you mentioned some things that occurred college; one that was the worst and another that was the best thing to ever happen. Can you explain?"

"Sure," Jim said. Taking a thoughtful sip of

coffee, the old man paused for a moment of reflection and begun…

"It was at the end of my first year at the University of Maine at Machias. I had enrolled in the college's four-year Bachelor of Science program and planned to earn a teaching certificate. With the University's credentials I hope to teach outdoor sciences. The winter had passed and with only two more weeks of classes; time was growing near to be out of school for the summer.

"A fellow student had spent the previous winter making a new cedar strip canoe so he and I talked about using the craft on a voyage down the Allagash. Open water meant it was time for us to prepare for our adventure. We'd heard that the wilderness trip was demanding, so my friend and I decided to do one final test on local rapids, to make sure the canoe was seaworthy. Near the college there was a small watercourse called the East Machias River, where we could give the canoe a final run after the last class.

"The day was Friday and the weather was bright and sunny as spring did its best to get through the month of April. There were still several hours of daylight so this was the time to do the practice river trip. Driving down Route 191 our subcompact car was an odd sight with the 17-foot canoe perched on the roof rack of a 14-foot- long Ford Escort.

"Parking the car in a wide spot off to the side of the paved way, upstream of a nearby bridge crossing; we realized that we'd forgotten our lifejackets. But that was ok, we thought, because both of us were excellent swimmers, and we were only going to canoe a very short ways. Surely we would be back to the college cafeteria in time for supper.

"While carrying the watercraft to the river, my friend casually mentioned 'If anything happens; the keys to the vehicle are in the ashtray.' At the time, I laughed off his declaration and thought, *what could possible happen*?

"The ice had just gone out of Hadley's Lake, a tributary to the river. The water was extremely high from the ice melt and the water temperature was estimated to be 36 degrees. After the canoes had been launched into the water, just above the bridge, we looked at each other, nodded our heads as if to declare, *let's do this*!

"At first bouncing down the rapids was fun, but when we passed under the bridge, the flow increased and a force of the water pushed the canoe toward the river left and a massive concrete abutment. We struggled valiantly to escape and had almost made it to calmer water, when suddenly waves ricocheted off the gray buttress and struck the canoe broadside. The wall of water hit the craft and shoved the boat into the middle of a boiling cross current. Consumed by whitecaps, the boat rolled, upended and threw us overboard. The undercurrent carried us with such energy that within a minute we'd been sped 50 feet downstream, *God the water is cold*! We hollered as both of us struggled to hold onto the sides of the swamped craft.

"When the boat finally drifted into calmer water, downstream from the overpass but still in the middle of the river; my friend and I decide to try for shore. He swam toward the south side of the river and I headed to the closer north embankment. When we parted, I heard my partner shriek, "No! Come this way!" Treading water, I looked back over my shoulder and saw the bright red face of my friend; but there was 20 feet of raging ice cold whitewater between us.

"In order to join my 'pal' I'd have to swim back through the center of the angry rollers; but dry land to the north was nearer. So I decided to keep swimming toward the closest bank where; once on dry ground, I could run through a field and cross the bridge to my companion.

"I waved at my partner and hollered, 'I'll see you on the other side,' and headed for the nearby dry ground. Swimming, hand over hand, seemingly for an eternity, I swam overhand at a snail's pace to reach the shoreline where I'd run across the bridge and to the aid of my companion. But dry land now seemed far away, the river was extremely cold and I felt sooo tired. Suddenly I looked down into the water and there, on the bottom of the river, I saw a queen-size bed with sheets turned down, just like my mom used to do when I was young.

"All I had to do was stop swimming and rest. Just a short but warm rest, then I could go to my friend. But, no, that wasn't possible. He needed help now!

"Fighting fatigue, I kept swimming, at a crawl, moving a few inches at a time. Hypothermia took control and soon my arms and legs were numb. Traumatized, I realized I'd reached the shallows only when my hand got tangled in the shore grass.

"Drenched to the bone, I crawled out of the water on hands and knees, and continued on all fours until my limbs warmed enough so I could stand. On shaky legs, I hobbled the remaining 50 feet to the road and crossed the highway crossing to the river's south side.

"Once there, I headed back to the water. When I started down the road embankment, I lost my balance and rolled down a small hill toward the water, all the while calling out to my friend as I tumbled.

"I finally made it to the flooding river, and waded back out into the cold water, but my feet and legs were so numb I couldn't feel the ice water anymore. I plodded out into the edge of current, the water climbed up to my waist as I called, called, and called to my partner and my friend: '**where are you? Where are you?**' But there was no answer. The only movement was the wave action of the river, splashing onto my belly and the current tugging at my belt as if inviting *let's go for a swim, shall we*?

"I never saw my friend again. That is until the day of his funeral."

Finished with scribing, Margaret looked deeply at Jim and sympathized, "That's terrible." Jim only nodded and a brief silence fell between the reporter and the interviewee as each one silently reflected about the unpredictability of life.

Remembering Jim's earlier statement and wanting to turn the discussion to a more positive mood, Margaret asked the follow-up question, "What was the best thing that ever happened?"

Moving to shake off a bad memory, Jim shifted in his chair and recalled brighter days, "It was the fall after the accident, during my sophomore year when I met Susan, the girl who eventually became my wife. At the time I was waiting in line at the water fountain for the student in front of to finish getting her drink. Speech class had just been dismissed and my next class wasn't due to start for another 15 minutes–so I had time to dawdle. The undergraduate at the fountain turned towards me and that when I looked into the deepest hazel green eyes I'd ever seen. But that wasn't all. Her teeth were pearly white, and she had shiny black hair that framed a face the sun had tanned to a radiant bronze. As pretty as she was, it was the eyes— her hypnotic eyes that immobilized me, and they have ever since, for the 50 plus years we've been married.

"After a bit, we started dating. I didn't have a car so we walked everywhere, covered the whole town of Machias, we did. We hadn't dated very long when my dad got sick and my parents couldn't make the trip to pick me up at school, so I bought my first car.

"The vehicle was blue; an almost deep blue

Mercury Comet, Susan said it was the prettiest car she'd ever seen." Reminiscing Jim allowed a smile to cross his lips and continued, "I particularly liked the way the automobile handled. I could drive with one hand on the steering wheel and, by the way, the car had a very good radio. The transportation opened doors to Washington County landmarks like beautiful Roque Bluffs State Park. There visitors can experience a pastel scene where the splashing salty waves roll in over the sand beach, and are greeted by the sweet fragrance of wild roses that grow wild on the nearby dunes.

"Then there was one-half mile long Jasper Beach. The gravel seashore was composed of fine-grained red volcanic rock that was so polished by the Atlantic, the stones gleamed in early morning light. Strolling along a beach of colored pebbles wasn't easy walking, but the surges of tide choreographed a constant clicky-clack, clicky-clack, clicky-clack as the ocean's salt waves moved the stones back and forth, made the effort worthwhile.

"And we laughed, laughed a lot actually. One evening I even tried singing to Susan. Now my mom used to say 'I couldn't carry a tune in a bucket.' But one night I'd grown tired of cramming for the big test scheduled for the next day. So I decided to walk over to see what Susan was up to. It was after curfew and I knew the front door would be locked, so I moved around the brick building and onto the parking lot at the back of the girls' dorm.

Staring at the building's second story I saw that the light in Susan's room was still on. Throwing a pebble at the windowpane to get her attention, she opened the window and scolded me for coming over so late.

" 'What do you want at this hour, Mister Clark?' She'd reprimanded with good humor.

"I'm tired of studying and so thought I drop by to say hi."

" 'Well—hi.' Susan said and smiled.' "

'Have you ever heard me sing?" I asked.

" 'Yes,' said Susan, 'but please don …' And before she could finish I broke out in a stanza of my favorite Hank Williams song. I was absorbed in the music and singing with my head up and eyes closed, I didn't even see Susan's roommate join her at the window. The two females whispered, smiled and disappeared. I never got the chance to finish. As quick as scat, the girls returned with a pail of water and lifted it up to the windowsill. Once in place, Susan and her roommate each grabbed a side of the bucket and threw the water as hard as they could at me—the forlorn-sounding singer below. The splash hit straight on, drenching me and drowning out the music.

"The next day Susan felt so bad that she bought me a piece of fresh strawberry pie at the nearby Helen's Restaurant, a popular eatery.

"Sharing plans for the future, we discovered a mutual interest in the Maine outdoors. As a young girl Susan had been sickly, but then she discovered Girl Scouts and Camp Natarswi. The legendary camp positioned along the shores of Lower Togue Pond, was handily located near the southern entrance of Baxter State Park. At camp she learned outdoor skills in camping, cooking, how to handle a canoe, and grew strong from hiking around and over mile-high Mt. Katahdin. While Susan had been at the camp, I had been in the park with my uncle.

"Between classes, we compiled a list of hikes and canoe trips and top on our list was the seven-mile hike into the Park's Russell Pond Campground and to canoe the Allagash.

"But due to my dad's illness I ended up leaving school and going back to work on the farm. Susan and I drifted apart and I didn't see her again for a few years until we ran into each other on Allagash Lake."

Totally engaged, Margaret typed as fast as Jim spoke and asked, "How, why did you go to Allagash Lake?"

"I'd found a letter left by a deceased grandfather and the correspondence instructed me to go to *The Lake* to retrieve an heirloom that my gramps had left years before. Eventually I ended up getting a temporary ranger job and guess I was good enough that ultimately I was hired to work full time.*

"But the real story and the one that I think you'll find most interesting is the first winter I spent working in the woods as a Waterway Ranger. I didn't think I was gonna make it through."

But before Margaret could ask, their conversation was interrupted by Jim's nurse. "Mr. Clark, it's time for medicine, and you need to take it before you eat." The RN commanded, impatient that she had to tell him the same thing at the same time every day. *He's been here long enough that I shouldn't have to wet nurse him—I have to constantly remind him! Isn't it enough that I have 24 other patients to*

*For the full details about how Jim got to Allagash Lake see the book "Solace-Allagash Lake Reloaded by Tim Caverly. Published March 2015

care for?

"Ok, ok" Jim replied to the care worker and winked at Margaret when he spoke to the RN, "I always look forward to the little pills because they make me enjoy a nap during the evening news.

"What do you say we talk more in a day or so? I've probably bent your ear enough for one day," the old ranger offered.

Not wanting to miss a piece of a story that was building into a very complex tale; Margaret suggested, "If you don't mind, I'd like to come back in the morning?" and the writer fretted silently *at his age and with all the meds he's taking, I'd better get all the details I can, while I can.*

"Good enough," Jim said as rose to follow the nurse to her duty station. Margaret said, "I am headed that way too; I'll walk with you."

Reader's Notes:

6
DAMN GOVERNMENT

Margaret and Jim left the sitting room and chattered pleasantly as they strolled side by side down the hall. When they got to the door of the nurse's post Jim turned to enter. Not wishing to abandon his young guest in the corridor, Jim suggested that Margaret "Go back and grab a coffee for your ride home. They generally have a platter of fruit and cookies up for grabs."

By then a late crowd from the auditorium had caught up with the reporter, and neared the nurse's duty station. So Margaret allowed the residents to pass and then stepped in behind two elderly women who were last in line. One by one the crowd thinned and noisy conversation quieted as residents split off to individual apartments in preparation for dinner. Moving with the two ladies, Margaret listened as the senior females conversed about Jim's last performance.

"Ellen, did you like James's recent talk?" The first lady continued without waiting for a response from her friend. "I thought his speech was marvelous."

"Yes, it certainly was." Ellen replied, "I always enjoy Jim's stories and he never tells the same one twice. The man has definitely led an exciting life. And he is so handsome. I'm amazed Jim still has all his hair."

With a distant look in her eyes, the second lady dreamily gazed into space and mused, "He must have been something to tame in his younger days." She continued with a secret smile and said, "And I think I would have liked to have been the one that tamed him; but then again I can't remember why I would have wanted to." Here the ladies giggled with the high-pitched enjoyment of a joke they used often.

Margaret approached the day room to grab the suggested coffee; were she was greeted by a series of loud squeaks. Peering into the room she saw a solitary person sitting in a rocking chair too close to the television screen–every few minutes he'd rock the chair three times and then stop, lean forward, sit on the edge of the seat, and glare at the screen on the wall.

Drawing closer Margaret heard him announce "damn government, government be damned. I'll tell you the trouble, it's not the government. It's the complacent voters who don't pay attention, that's the problem!" The statement immediately captured the reporter's attention, so Margaret paused to hear what troubled the only other person in the room; the faster he rocked, the noisier the chair screeched.

Totally absorbed by the day's *breaking news from Maine's capital city*; the fellow stopped rocking and balanced again on the edge of his rocking chair. With bent arthritic knuckles, he struggled to grip the arms of the chair while the man stared in total concentration at the television's monitor. Curious Margaret moved closer to see what was on, as her father used to say, 'the tube' and to learn what had infuriated the old man.

Margaret couldn't help but briefly ponder, *wonder why dad called his TV the tube?* Forgetting her curiosity Margaret listened for the rocking chair man to answer the newscaster's question of, "and why isn't the government taking the measures necessary to resolve the horrific problems exposed by today's breaking news?"

"Any fool who pays attention knows that *we–the–people* are the government you damn fool!" the old man grumbled and rocked, with every back and forth movement, the chair's rockers squawked in protest. "If the government ain't taking proper actions, then it's the people's fault. Sure politicians are elected," the man ranted, "and they stand up real pretty and smile with store bought teeth for the camera. And there is no doubt that they will take credit for any good that happens and shift the blame for anything bad. It don't take very long for a reasonable observer to learn that the first responsibility of a politician is to be re-elected.

"'But for sure it is the duty of the American people to hold bad politicians answerable for their actions. Years ago even American humorist Will Rogers observed that the voting public didn't do very well at 'holdin' the politician accountable" 'the short memory of the American Voter is what keeps our politicians in Office,' Rogers had said.

"Oh sure there have been some good ones right here in Maine—never mind if they were Democrat, Republican, or Independent," Margaret continued to eavesdrop while the man argued with the TV and increased his chair's pace. The runners of the chair continued to object.

The reporter crept closer to hear the old man's wisdom while he lectured the large screen. Totally focused on the news, the old man did not hear her approach. "There are dozens who've cared about our state and the people in it. But there were some bad ones too; those who sought egotistical power and opportunities to enrich their own pockets. Yessir, those were the ones that give all legislators a bad name and appoint incompetents to serve as commissioners and directors. Anyone knows who they are—all a body gotta do is read the papers. Those are the so-called officials the Maine citizens should have kicked out on their butts." And then the editorial critic rocked some more. The interlocking joints of the chair's pleas for lubricant went un-noticed by the old man absorbed by the broadcast.

Finally hearing Margaret's footsteps, the man invited, without taking his eyes off the 24 hour news channel, "Sit down, if you want," and then capitalized his offer with a final outburst of "damn fools!"

Lowering the volume of the television; the man softened the tone of his voice only slightly and questioned, "You that woman reporter who's interviewing Jim?"

"Yes" the writer replied. "My name is Margaret," as she reached out with a right hand for a traditional greeting.

"Would love to shake but can't, hands hurt real bad. My joints are all stiff and sore, but never mind that. Heard you don't like to be called Maggie neither." The man stated in a matter-of fact way of speaking, not expecting a disagreement or a response; he continued with his opinion.

"He's not gonna tell ya, you know?"

"He not gonna tell me what?" Margaret questioned.

"About the vandalism and the political stuff!"

"Vandalism? Political stuff?"

"Never mind, shouldn't have mentioned anything." The old guy said as he used the TV's select control to increase the sound level of the news and drown out the topic he'd suggested; then he rocked some more. The rockers squeaked once more.

Grabbing the remote from its resting place from the arm of the chair; Margaret reduced the level of the anchor's analysis of the latest news to a whisper. The reporter, in order to get the man to talk, asked an interrelated question "How well do you know Jim?"

"Oh, pretty well I guess. I worked beside him

for years in the deepest part of the Maine woods," the old man stated

Sensing new information that might be significant for the interview, Margaret pressed the old-timer for more information. She soon learned that the old fellow's name was Matt and that he had worked along with and eventually directly for Jim.

Over the next hour Matt told how he too had been a ranger, and when the time came that Jim was promoted to Ranger Supervisor, Matt had stayed on in a year-round ranger job that he loved. It had been working in extreme conditions found in the spring, fall and winter that had caused the disfigurement which had crippled the old fellow's joints.

Soon one hour had passed and the conversation continued on. For two and a half hours Margaret heard how Jim's challenges had started the first year of his appointment to the Supervisor's position. The first day of work, Jim's predecessor had told him over coffee, about sabotage that had gone on for years.

Eventually the first administrator resigned figuring, as he had told Jim; "Maybe if I leave the destruction will stop before somebody gets hurt." And Margaret learned that the damage did stop for a while, but not before an arsonist burned the Supervisor's lodge—Jim's headquarters—to the ground.

Jim had accepted the job and he was immediately assigned the task of calming the turbulent wilderness. He'd also been instructed, as required by law, to establish goals to protect the wild and scenic corridor from pressures of development. But Jim hadn't been in the new job for more than a few years when the physical harm calmed, only to resume into political pressure as a powerful politician began to use his muscle to receive special privileges.

The first time Jim had learned about political influence was when the politician's favorite sporting camp within the wilderness area wanted to install a luxuriant hot tub. The statesman's tub was too close to the small pond where the camp was located and didn't meet legal setback requirements. So rather than cancel the plans for the lush amenity, the politician sent a formal letter on legislative stationery to the Land Use Regulatory Agency declaring that since the [hot tub] *didn't meet [the letter of the] law, then the state agency should change their law.*

Another instance was when the same politician wanted $100,000 from the state's general fund to build a road and camp within 600 feet of the wilderness canoe route. When Jim, as the field administrator opposed the construction, the ranger was threatened with legislation to make the state job a political appointee "to serve at the will of the Governor." When that intimidation didn't work, the same politician introduced a law to force Jim to live in the woods 12 months a year, which, if passed, would have meant the ranger-supervisor, would have been separated from his family for weeks at a time. Eventually calmer heads prevailed and a responsible legislator killed the bullying bills.

"Since 1966 there have been almost 50 pieces of legislation either introduced and/or passed to support one person or another's private agenda. Maybe the place would have been better off under federal control," Matt opined.

Matt also shared with Margaret that those were only a portion of the political muscle exerted, and if she wanted more evidence, then she should research an historic periodical called the *Maine Times*. *The Maine Times* investigative reporter," Matt said, "covered the issue extensively. As a further check you should review the files in the state's Department of Conservation office in Augusta. The agency should have (if they hadn't destroyed 'em) all the incidents reports on file."

Then in a much softer tone so as not to be over heard "Follow the money, if you want to know what and why stuff happened. Follow the money."

Totally intrigued, Margaret asked, "So tell me, Matt, why wouldn't Jim tell me about all of those clashes? The confrontations must have been very stressful."

"Yeah, they were. But he won't tell ya because Jim would see it as airing dirty laundry and he ain't one to complain. He's always preferred to remain positive. Jim will tell you about normal, everyday in the field challenges but that is as far as it would go. If you want to find out the whole story, you'll need to dig out the evidence."

Figuring he'd already said too much, Matt grabbed the remote and turned up the sound on the television and once again started talking to the commentator, "When you see someone saying they can't do something because it's the government fault they're just giving an excuse to not get involved. Why don't you report that?" The old man then offered one more quote from his favorite satirist, Will Rogers, "Ole Wil' also said that some men learn from readin', a few learn from observin' and then there are those who just have to pee on the electric fence to learn what happens." With that Matt rocked faster and the chair's rockers shrilled.

Thinking about the recent revelation, Margaret left the old man to his self-editorializing and left the facility to walk to her car and made a mental note *to web-search the Maine Times, pay a visit to the Augusta office of the Department of Conservation and to 'follow the money.'*

Margaret suddenly remembered the earlier episode with her vehicle and thought, *I hope it starts.* She never noticed that the pickup was gone.

Reader's Notes:

7
WELCOME TO CAMP

The next morning Margaret pulled into her customary space, well before her normal arrival time of 6:45. Walking behind the 4x4; the reporter noticed that the dusty truck had been washed and the tire repaired. *Wonder when that was done?*

Entering the portico she found Jim waiting, and holding the door open. He smiled when he saw Margaret and handed her a cup of coffee with a splash of cream and three sugars—ingredients he'd watched her add during their last visit. Surprised to find the old ranger standing at the entrance; some distance from his customary seat, she accepted the hot mug of bitter liquid.

Eagerly Jim said, "Here's your coffee just the way you like it. Come on, come on we've got stuff to look at, let's head to my room; muffins are waiting, hope you're hungry."

Following Jim as he shuffled at double speed through the lobby Margaret saw that the dayroom was full to the brim with activities. Halfway down the hall Jim pointed to a door and said, "This is my room. Come in, come in!"

Looking at the door Margaret noticed there was a placard that proclaimed *Welcome to Jim's Cabin*. Under the sign was a carved hand-painted picture of a trapper's cabin that sat elevated on a knoll above the waterline of a turquoise colored lake. In the landscape, the porch of the camp was close enough to the water so a person could cast a fish line from the veranda. A clump of white birch trees graced the property near the edge of the porch. A whitetail deer peeked around a red pine, a green canoe waited on the beach while soft white smoke drifted out of the chimney.

Waving at the door decoration, Jim probed, "Do you like it?" Without waiting for an answer, he continued, 'My daughter had that done, as well as the decorations in the room. I love my boys, but of all my children it is my daughter, Isabella, who acts the most like me. When a little girl she was my shadow, went everywhere with me; Bella was in my canoe so much

I called her my bow weight. Come in, come in. Leave the door open, so busybodies won't talk."

Walking inside Margaret couldn't believe her eyes. If the reporter didn't know different, she would have thought she was entering a home located deep in the Alaskan wilderness.

Passing by the door to an apartment bathroom on the right, Margaret entered a single room, decorated to replicate a one-room log cabin. The first thing she noticed was the flat had been painted a light tan to replicate a softwood finish, a texture that gave the room a warm glow. Cream-colored, cotton curtains draped over the dwelling's only window, portrayed wintery scenes of Maine wildlife. Outside, songbirds grouped around a squirrel feeder. Centered on the wall directly opposite the window, a 38-40 caliber Marlin Rifle rested on a gun rack under the 12-point taxidermy mount of a whitetail. Kerosene lamps, adapted for electricity, were arranged about the room for light and aesthetics.

A double bed against one wall was covered by a decorative pine tree quilt. Two feather pillows, in red pillow cases were arranged for a nap, or, a night's sleep. An antique, golden oak rolltop desk with matching captain's chair waited for someone to take a seat and scribe in a diary. Standing diagonal in the corner halfway between the desk and the window stood a miniature Kineo Princess Model woodstove.

The cookstove, once used to bake beans,

Tim having a conversation about foxes with a Spruce Grouse at the Tramway.
Photograph from the Tim Caverly Collection.

Robert the Bobcat waiting patiently for lunch.
Photograph from the Tim Caverly Collection.

biscuits, and apple pies, now served the sole purpose of accommodating a vase of flowers and as a display area for a collection of Indian artifacts, recovered from their resting place below a high-water line. Pointing at a stone axe, Jim said, "That was found on Chamberlain Lake in six inches of water. At the time archaeologists estimated the ancient tool to be about 5,000 years old. My collection will all go to the state office of historic preservation someday, that's where it belongs; proper."

Strolling around the room Margaret found a life's collection of pictures, awards, and recognitions of every shape and size. There were winter pictures of animals; a photograph of a bobcat, a ranger holding a spruce grouse, and an aerial view of Allagash Lake.

There was also a conservation plaque from Ducks Unlimited recognizing James P. Clark as the Katahdin Area Chairperson of the Year, and a framed letter from Maine's Governor, congratulating Jim on his retirement. A gray moose horn hung on the wall. A silhouette of the state of Maine had been carved into the antler's palm. There were framed historic photographs such as the towboat *H.W. Marsh.*

"Sitting of the keel" of the towboat H.W. Marsh at the Chamberlain Lake end of the Tramway. Photograph from the Terry Harper Collection

W.H. Marsh under operation. Photograph from the Terry Harper Collection.

But what drew Margaret's attention was a letter displayed on top of the rolltop desk, displayed in a bronze frame. Picking up the frame, Margaret read...

Maine Department of Conservation
Bureau of Parks and Lands
Allagash Wilderness Waterway
P.O. Box 365
Millinocket, Maine 04462

Mr. James Clark, Allagash Ranger
P.O. Box 626
Clayton Lake, Maine 04737

Dear Jim,

I am writing to express my appreciation for your work in the Allagash Lake District over these past years. Your attention to detail and extreme resourcefulness when faced with unknown situations that need immediate attention is recognized and appreciated.

Because of your obligation to duty, I am pleased to offer you a year-round position, where during the winter you'll live at Churchill Dam and Chamberlain Bridge–as needed. As we discussed last week, you are assigned to move into the ranger's camp by Nov. 14 and work from there until May 1; when you are scheduled to report back to the Allagash Lake District.

Your duties will include assignments all along the 92 mile length of the Waterway and you'll discover that the cold weather operations are quite demanding. I am confident that you have the personal resources, resilience, and stamina necessary to fulfill your duties while working in extreme arctic conditions.

Sincerely,

Leigh

Leigh Smith, Superintendent

While she read, Jim explained. "The two years before I received that letter had been a difficult time. First my dad died, which forced me to leave college and my girlfriend, Susan, behind. Then my mom got sick and passed away. The farm got into financial trouble and just when I didn't know what to do I found a letter from my grandfather. My Pépé died a couple of months before I was born. But he knew I was on the way so he wrote me a letter with instructions it be delivered on my 21st birthday. But my parents passed away before they could give it to me. In the correspondence I found instructions to go to Allagash Lake to retrieve an heirloom my grandfather had left years before.

"To make a long story short, I ended up at the lake, and while there I learned about my family history, and discovered an 1838 copper penny with the initials JPC engraved into the coin's face. The one cent turned out to be magical and it opened unexpected doors to an event."

Totally absorbed, Margaret sat in the oak desk chair mesmerized as Jim took a seat in an overstuffed chair and continued with an almost unbelievable story.

"I found the coin the same night that a mass of fireflies swarmed in over Allagash Lake. The flight came fast until they landed along the edges of the trail to the Ice Caves. I followed their trail uphill to the caverns where I found …"

Three hours later, after multiple cups of coffee Jim finished his tale with, "And so I asked Susan to marry me and then I was appointed to a full-time ranger's position. And that's the story behind the letter."

Scribing furiously, Margaret recorded everything Jim had said when he suggested, "What do you say we continue tomorrow, the nurse will be here in a few minutes and she'll interrupt us anyway."

Margaret got up to leave, and noticed, for the first time, the pictures on the wall by his bed. About head high, on the wall in a place of prominence were two photographs. One image was of a family standing in front of a brown, cedar-shingled camp. Recognizing the image of a younger Jim Clark proudly wearing a ranger's uniform, she saw that Jim had his right arm around the shoulders of a shorter, attractive lady with a dazzling smile, coal black hair and hazel green eyes. *Pretty woman* Margaret thought. Standing, centered in front of the couple there were three children of assorted ages; two boys and a girl. The youngest, the miss, appeared to be about five years old. Beside the little child sat a golden retriever staring up adoringly at the ranger. Beside the family portrait was a photograph of a single man standing in a canoe holding a canoe pole. "Is that your family?" Margaret asked.

"Yes, taken many years ago at the Allagash Lake camp. That's my wife, Susan; oldest son, Jim Jr.; middle child, George; and my little girl, Bella. The dog was my third golden and her name was Misty. The picture to the right of my family is of Dalton James. He was a close friend of my gramps and introduced me to the deep woods and Allagash

Lake; great man with a great family. Every once in a while Dalton's grandson Dennis stops by. He works as a game warden in the unorganized townships. Hope you get a chance to meet him sometime. He takes my current dog, Sandi, with him from time to time."

"Beautiful family," Margaret offered ignoring the single picture of Dalton James and the suggestion of meeting the grandson. Then with memories of her own starting to well up into her eyes, she focused on the balanced family portrait and thought *if I didn't know any better I'd swear the little girl in the picture was me, she looks identical to a picture my mom had of our family when I was little.* Wanting to put the thought out of her mind, Margaret grabbed her coat off the bed and turned to look at another picture on the wall beside the door to the bathroom.

The silver framed depiction was a winter scene of a coyote chasing a deer on the opposite side of a river. Jim noticed her looking at the picture and he captured the reporter's attention with, "That was taken my first winter on the job by a close friend and his wife.

* Author's Note: For more information about Dalton James, see the book Allagash Tails Volume 6 "Solace."

Coyote stalking a whitetail along Chase Rapids in 1992 Photograph by Dean Bennett.

A winter that offered so many experiences and dangers; I am not sure there are enough words on your machine to write 'em all down. But we'll talk about all that tomorrow."

Before Margaret got through the door of the apartment, Jim picked up a cardboard box full of red hardcover logbooks. Each book measured five inches by seven inches and had Algerian letters embossed in gold which identified them as **JOURNALS**. Under the title, in similar gold lettering were Arabic numerals that specified the year that each diary represented.

"I'll lug these out to your vehicle for ya."

"What are they?"

"Ranger logs and assorted papers I've collected

over time. The journals are pages where I recorded my daily experiences. You'll find that the diaries are all there, one for each year I worked. I think there might be some information you'll find interesting."

Walking to her car and wishing to avoid any subject of family, Margaret pointed at the brown truck parked beside her car and asked, "What's the story with the pickup? It's always parked there, no matter when I come."

"No story really, it's my truck."

"Yours! Do you drive?"

"Only a little and I'm required to return before dark. The home allows me to keep it. Having the truck outside makes me think I can go to the woods whenever I want, but I know I'm supposed to stay here. I drive it around town once in a while, just to turn the tires, but I have to give the keys to the receptionist whenever I return. Eventually my son will come and take it away."

Sliding behind the steering wheel of her car, Margaret smiled and waved goodbye at her friend and pleasantly said she would return in the morning. She waited for Jim to hobble away on sore knees before starting her vehicle. Once the old ranger was out of sight, Margaret engaged the engine so others couldn't hear. Unable to contain her feelings any longer this independent, resourceful, hardnosed reporter—cried.

Reader's Notes:

8
HER FAMILY

Fighting to regain composure, Margaret battled tears all the way back to her rent on the river. But once inside the privacy of her apartment a flood of waterworks gushed from the recesses of her mind. She'd been fine until she'd witnessed the warmth of Jim's replicated cabin, the picture of a happy family and the feeling of kinfolk that brought on recollections from the past.

She placed the *oddly heavy* box of Jim's diaries onto the room's dual purpose kitchen table and work station; Margaret thought that Jim's room had looked just like a cabin she used to visit with her father when very young. And the picture, it was the picture that had put her over the emotional edge. At one time she'd had a happy childhood, memories which were quietly fading, memoirs she fought desperately to hold onto.

An only child, Margaret never really knew her biological father, who had been orphaned. Margaret had never met her mother's father nor had she seen that many pictures of him. Margaret's mom had said that despite a difficult childhood, Margaret's real dad had been a kind man and someone who loved trips into the Maine woods. Margaret had heard that her grandfather had been involved in an accident when he was young which had damaged his face, so he didn't like to have his picture taken. Margaret's mother, as Margaret had learned, did have a few pictures of the grandfather's "good side" but they didn't really show all of his features.

Margaret's mother had loved her father and had tried to marry someone like him; which she had found in Margaret's dad. The mom had met her first husband late in life and the couple was happy and very excited when Margaret had been born. The couple loved their little girl and took her everywhere. The mom had said that baby Margaret had brought a breath of spring into the fall of her husband's life.

But when Margaret turned six her dad died from a severe heart attack. The mom needed the income a second marriage would bring; so she wed a man who soon turned into someone quite different from the person she'd dated. Not long after the new husband moved into Margaret's home and to the mother's bed, he made it clear that he didn't like kids.

"Miss Maggie Magoo," as he referred to his wife's daughter, commanded that "Maggie wasn't to talk during meals and that the young'un was to come right home after school to do dishes, laundry, and housecleaning. And by the way, Miss Maggie," he'd grinned "just so you'll know; I'm gonna manage any dough you might ever earn. That is if you can ever find anyone who will even think of hiring ya!" Margaret hadn't like the look in the man's eyes when he talked about money, or about managing her affairs.

The new husband forced his 'wifey' to get a job as a bar waitress and she was expected to turn over any income and tips at the end of each work shift. The man needed money for beer, cigarettes, and for those places where he disappeared each night.

Margaret didn't know for sure, but suspected the husband beat her mom whenever he felt like it. Her mother would never admit it, and never ever told Margaret's uncles, but every once in a while the outline of a bruise on the side of her mother's face would show through her ever-thickening make-up.

The only relief that the little girl would get

was when her mom's brothers would take Margaret fishing, hiking, and camping. But when she returned home, no matter how long she'd been gone her stepdad would always greet her with, "Well Miss Magoo, you've returned already. Wasn't any reason to hurry back you know!"

The little girl hated the nicknames and felt *such labels only serve to purposely hurt others.* Other than her days at school, Margaret's childhood was a miserable existence. When she turned 18, Margaret's mom died of heartbreak. Now that her mother no longer needed the daughter's protection, and her stepfather who *she refused to call daddy* suddenly realized that Margaret could be real handy, the girl wanted out.

Fortunately Margaret's teacher, Mrs. Stetson, came to the student's aid. The educator had seen something in Margaret that others hadn't, and encouraged the student to apply for college.

"But what would I study in school?" Margaret had asked her favorite teacher and the dedicated educator had replied, "You write excellent compositions. I'd suggest going after a teaching or a journalism degree. I think you have the ability to eventually publish a book."

Margaret applied for and was accepted to the University of Maine at Orono. Leaning toward journalism so she could improve her writing skills, but remembering the good times she had in the woods in her early childhood, Margaret decided on a major in journalism with minors in forestry and biology. "While a writing career is good, it is also practical to have other options," her science teacher, Mr. Johnson, had suggested.

Working night and day, Margaret worked her way through college, never seeing her stepfather again. Margaret was considered by many to be fetching and was often asked for a date. But her work-study and course regiment consumed her time and energy. Many a late night Margaret arrived back to her room only to collapse exhausted into bed.

Except for her roommate, Margaret didn't have any friends and cared less about socializing with the opposite sex. In her opinion, there were too many men like her mother's second husband prowling around the courting world.

But now that she had time to herself, in the evenings and days off the girl was lonely. Margaret's uncles lived far away and were busy with their own careers and families. The private woman missed that sense of having close loved ones that so many of her coworkers enjoyed. The solitary life was worse on Thanksgiving and Christmas. She didn't even have a cat or dog waiting when she returned to the room that overlooked the Penobscot. And to top it all off—she was broke. *And those memories had all come back— thanks to that damn picture.*

*****

To regain self-control and think about something else while waiting for her evening pot of tea to steep, Margaret turned to the box of books that Jim had provided.

Opening the first diary Margaret read:

From the diary of James Clark
The Ranger and the Reporter
The deep woods of northern Maine are 'out of the way.' Not just remote but so withdrawn there aren't any formal settlements or cities, only unorganized townships-measuring six miles by six miles—these 36 square miles of pure timberlands are identified on maps by letters and numbers. In Township 7

Range 13, you aren't in the middle of nowhere, but you can sure see it from there.

In T7R13, as it is abbreviated, there is a state campground on the shore of the prettiest stream you'll ever see. The tributary, known as Ellis Brook drains a large forest area to the northwest and brings clear, cool water to 18-mile-long Chamberlain Lake. It is a brook abundant with history and full of life.

If you listen to old-timers they will tell tales of a bygone era. Of a time when the locomotives of the West Branch and Eagle Lake Railroad roared south over the brook as the trains hauled pulp southwest to Umbazooksus Lake; Where once parked at the lakeside terminus, rail cars were relieved of their load and timber floated into the watershed of the west branch of the Penobscot River on its way to become fodder for the paper mills in Millinocket and beyond.

Guides will tell you about the time

Al Nugent of Nugent's Sporting Camp took Maine Governor Ken Curtis miles up the stream to a secret fishing hole that Nuge discovered one year when beaver trapping; and how both returned with their limit of ten of the prettiest pound and a half to three pound brook trout that a person could ever see.

Seasoned woodsmen might even tell you 'bout the time a big city reporter came up to interview spring fishermen about their open-water adventure. The correspondent had planned ahead. A month before the journalist had made arrangements through the supervisor of the Allagash Wilderness Waterway. The boss instructed his subordinate to boat her the eight miles to Ellis Brook campsite where a party of several men had settled in.

Early one May morning, the ranger and the reporter left the warmth of the ranger station at Chamberlain Bridge and boated through the frosty spring air in a 17-foot Boston Whaler powered by a 70-horsepower outboard. Under power, the Whaler cut cleanly through mirror calm water.

The woman reporter, more accustom to sitting at a desk than confronting chilly spring temperatures, put her back to the wind to avoid facing the brisk airstream flowing over the bow.

When she turned, she saw something that most visitors to nearby popular Baxter Park never see, the snow-covered north side of Katahdin in the early purple splendor of a spring day.

Arriving at the campsite, initially the scene was of an idyllic camping picture. There was a large, green, canvas bivouac tent; smoke curled above a fireplace, a person stood at the picnic table, cooking over a propane stove. The smell of frying bacon drifted across the water. It was a sight that presented the perfect recreational portrait, suitable for framing. But nearing shore the ranger and reporter discovered something totally different.

When the ranger throttled back the outboard, the motor quieted so the two could hear the commotion coming from the campsite and beyond.

First they heard the echo of laughter, when the baying of a beagle interrupted the sound of enjoyment. Looking up, the ranger and the reporter saw the hunting dog running through the woods, snapping at the heels of a doe deer. Immediately the ranger knew this might not be a good experience for his correspondent.

Tying the boat off to a nearby tree, the two walked into the campsite. There were six men gathered about in a variety of activities, most of which involved early morning drinking. The ground was littered with containers of empty beer cans, glass whiskey bottles, plastic rum bottles, there was even a discarded half-gallon jug of Jose Cuervo; which was missing the Maguey worm.

Seeing a lady in the boat, two of the men approached to say welcomed. The reporter introduced herself and explained the reason for her visit, and the campers agreed to be interviewed. But her first question brought an uncomfortable response.

"What are you fishing for?" the reporter inquired.

"Anything we can catch" came the immediate reply.

"Such as?" she inquired searching for complete answers to her questions.

"Brook trout, togue, whitefish, and smelts mostly" they replied.

"Have you been able to catch any fish?"

"Oh yes!" came the reply as they pointed to a cooler full of fish. "We're getting dozens of togue, brook trout, and whitefish every time we go out. Come take a look. We were just getting ready to go back onto the lake again."

Then she stated, "Nice looking mess of fish." Here the ranger interrupted with a question of his own, "Do you guys know what the daily bag limit is?"

Suddenly the fishermen realized that the ranger was wearing a badge that displayed his law enforcement status. The group got very nervous and answered, "Oh yes and we are within our limit. And we are all done fishing for the day."

While the park ranger began separating and counting the game fish, one of the campers, who had been sleeping, heard the female voice and staggered from one of the tents. Through bloodshot eyes, he spied the pretty lady and asked, "You look cold, do you wanna lay down for a while? I am feeling sleepy and I could keep you warm."

With a politeness that the crowd didn't deserve, she replied, "No, I am pregnant and feel fine right here."

The man didn't want to take no for an answer, so he persisted with, "that's ok, I don't mind sleeping with a lady who has a bun in the oven."

Waving him away, the reporter turned to speak with a man who seemed more sober than the others. After finishing her interview, the ranger and the reporter turned to head up the lake to check the next campsite.

The reporter got her story, and the campers got a few presents of their own, three in all. Summonses to court for allowing their dog to chase deer, for littering, and for over their limit of fish.

But the real story is Ellis Brook. The stream is clean and cold and a great place to net the spring run of freshwater smelt. But what comes into the stream after the smelts leave is where the real tale lies.

The smelt run is dependent on the spring melt, water levels, and temperatures. After the smelts have finished their run to the spawning ground, the common suckers will come into the brook to do their spring breeding. These bottom-feeders with fleshy papillose lips can grow up to 6 pounds and 20 inches long. While in the brook, the suckers will eat algae, plant matter, organic matter, and small insects. They serve as the small aquatic vacuum cleaners for the brook.

In the spring, a female sucker will carry up to 10,000 eggs and when there is a school of fish, if you take a closer look, you might find brook trout. Several times I've seen a big brookie swim among the suckers and as they go, the brook trout will slap the sides of the suckers with their tails. The suckers are so over-loaded with eggs that when they are hit by the square tails the eggs of the female sucker are released, which the trout scoff up.

Margaret enjoyed the May entry so she decided to skip ahead and peruse a November entry–in order to determine if the entertaining style of the story line continued.

From the diary of James Clark Stormy

Boy what a summer! There's so much going on the journal entries have come fast and furious, the pages are almost full. In a ranger's job, it doesn't take long to understand that every day is different and there are many 15 hour days in a week.

My wife and I are temporary staying at the headquarters on Umsaskis Lake and last night my first on-the-job search and rescue mission occurred. It's the third week of November and the state is in the middle of its yearly deer hunting season.

The day began innocently enough. I'd had driven the 70 plus miles to Ashland to meet with state agencies and paper company foresters. Susan had remained behind to take care of her secretarial duties.

I had planned to head back into the woods by 2 P.M. but the appointments took longer than expected, so I didn't get back into the truck until almost dark.

By 5:30 P.M. I had only driven halfway to the cabin and was tired, and hungry for the hot supper that I knew was waiting. All day the thermometer had hovered around 40 degrees but with the darkness a full moon appeared and temperatures fell. At 33 degrees, the Lakes hadn't frozen, but there was an arctic chill in the air.

By the time I was an hour from camp thick clouds had obscured the moon. The headlights of my 4x4 cut through the pitch black night when suddenly my ranger's two-way radio crackled.

"Umsaskis to 1700," Susan was calling me.

I immediately keyed my microphone and replied, "10-3 (go ahead), Umsaskis."

"I hear gun-shots outside; I think a hunter might be lost or in trouble."

"10-4 (I copied), Susan. Can you tell the direction from where the shots are coming?"

"It sounds like over Priestly Mountain way, near the fire watchman's tower."

"My ETA is about 40 minutes and we'll see if we can figure out what's going on."

"10-4, I'll wait at camp."

"10-4, see you in travel time" I confirmed.

30 minutes later I drove in the yard, and arrived at my cabin only to find the residence in complete darkness. I thought it odd that Susan didn't have the kitchen lights on. When I shut my truck off, she met me at the door with a flashlight in hand.

"How come the generator isn't running and the power turned on?" I inquired worried that maybe the equipment had broken down and she had been alone in the darkness.

Susan anxiously replied, "That's when I heard the gunfire–when I turned our house lights on. To me it sounded like the firing came from the ridge to the southwest."

"Go ahead and start the generator and snap on the entryway lights. I'll walk to the shore to see if I can hear anything away from the noise of the power plant."

By the time I got to the waterline, Susan had the generator running and the porch's 100-watt bulbs lite up the night. Immediately a volley of rifle fire came from the other side of the lake. The gunshots Susan had heard were echoes from the lake's east side.

I ran to camp and hollered, "I think I know about where the shots are coming from. I'm going to grab my bear rifle and shoot into the air to let whoever it is know we've heard 'em. Shut off the generator," I instructed.

Once inside I grabbed my 30-30 Winchester model 94 and with carbine in hand, I ran back out onto the porch and discharged three rounds into the eerie night. My shots were immediately answered by three volleys from across the lake.

The previous summer, I had flown over that township and saw there wasn't a road near that side of the lake. So I told Susan, "I'll have to get the 20-foot Grumman canoe and Mercury outboard out of storage. Looks like I've gotta cross the lake; someone must be in trouble. I hope they aren't hurt."

About that time the wind increased and snow started to swirl. Susan said, "I am going too. You may need help." Realizing she was right, I didn't argue and just nodded and replied "leave the front porch lights on so we can find our way back. Put on your cold weather gear and lifejacket, it's starting to snow.

Let's grab the first aid kit, my compass, extra life jackets, and our five-cell flashlights."

Within a short time we launched the canoe; me in the stern and Susan on her knees in the bow—a husband and wife team motoring across Umsaskis Lake, in the middle of November, in the middle of a snowstorm, in the middle of darkness. The wind howled and the snow flurries swelled into a full-fledge squall.

Motoring across the lake, we heard the purring of the outboard, the train-like roar of a nor'easter on the way while waves of freezing water smacked the sides of the aluminum craft. Whitecaps banged the canoe like a spoon beating on a tin can.

Void of any light I used my flashlight to read the compass. The magnetic pull on the instrument's needle kept us heading in a straight line.

In the bow, while Susan scanned the darkness for sign of land, I had to yell to be heard over the night sounds. "Turn on your flashlight and keep it trained over the front of the canoe. Let's try and pick out the east shore." Immediately flurries cut across the flashlight's beam and I could see that our paddles, lifejackets, and gunnels were covered white with powder.

As soon as Susan turned on her lantern we saw an illumination flare from the far shore. I took a new compass bearing and turned the canoe straight for the fleeting light.

Then another blaze flared, and then a third and a fourth. After the sixth flash we saw a match strike and a small object burn briefly. Then the metal keel of our canoe screeched in protest as it skidded to a stop on a flat rock. We had crossed the two-mile wide lake and beached on the eastern shore.

Directly in front of us we saw

a man standing silent, staring, not believing what emerged from the storm. He was missing his hat and shivered uncontrollably. His orange hung tattered, and he carried his rifle by a death-like grip.

I asked, "Are you alone?"

He just gaped with mouth open.

I asked again, louder, "Is there anyone with you?"

The hunter shook his head no. So I said, "well, welcome aboard, let's go get some coffee." With the invitation he smiled, limped to our canoe, and escape from the dark forest.

Just in time to as it turned out. The hunter had tracked a deer all day, gotten lost, and had walked miles in the wrong direction.

When Susan had turned on the camp lights, the hunter had fired to get our attention. The intermittent blazes we'd seen had been the lost man burning everything in his wallet. By the time we arrived, he'd run out of ammunition and set fire to his last 20 dollars. The huntsman had planned to return to his camp before dark and so had not bothered carrying a flashlight. He had just used his last match signaling for help.

Other than being extremely wet and cold; the hunter was ok. Once he was seated in the canoe, I turned the -20- footer with the wind, and with the snow and wind now at our backs we motored west across the lake, carried along by cresting waves of water. In an hour, we'd returned to the welcome warmth of our cabin.

After cups of coffee and a hot meal, I drove our visitor the ten miles to his camp. His friends were sure tickled to see him. It was a situation that ended ok, but if Susan hadn't turned on our kitchen lights and hadn't heard his gun-shots; he might still be in the forest today.

Finishing the evening tea with just a squeeze of lemon and feeling better, Margaret thumbed through several of the diaries, and noticed something very odd.

Reader's Notes:

9
JIM'S CLAN

The next morning Margaret arrived back at Pleasant Ridge in preparation for that day's interview. Margaret pulled into her usual parking space and observed a man securing a black steel-framed canoe rack onto Jim's truck. Placing her car's transmission in park; the reporter studied the stranger working on her subject's vehicle.

The man appeared to be near middle age. Wearing a ball cap, green sweater, dungarees, and hiking boots, the person moved effortlessly from one side of the pickup to the other. Inside the pickup a golden retriever sat and watched every movement of Margaret's arrival, and wagged her tail waiting for any opportunity to make a new friend or get a treat.

Exiting her car and curious about the visitor, the

reporter stopped to make conversation. "Is this your truck?" Margaret asked secure in the knowledge that it wasn't.

"No," was the reply. "Who's asking?" the newcomer suspiciously probed.

Margaret stuck out her hand and introduced herself, "My name is Margaret Woodward "and I'm a..."

"The reporter, interviewing my dad," completed the man. Smiling he said, "Hi, my name is George, and Jim is my father. Pleased to meet you. I've been hearing good things about you."

"Really?" Margaret replied. Jim had been playing his cards close to his chest and she hadn't been sure he liked her questions or prying to open the doors to his past.

"Yes, he's been expecting you this morning and said that he's enjoying the reminiscing. Go ahead in. He made me buy some fresh baked doughnuts from the bakery, he and they are waiting. I'll be in shortly. I'm almost finished. By the way," the son continued, "have you thought to have a mechanic look at the tires on your car?"

"No, why?" Margaret wondered why he was asking such a strange question.

"Well, your front tires look a little worn. You may want to have a garage look at 'em. Appears like you'll need to replace at least one."

"Sure, thanks for noticing," Margaret replied as she thought. *Great! Just what I need is another bill— heck I can't pay what I owe now.* Then she ended the conversation with, "I'll have them checked as soon as I can," then turned and walked toward the building.

Continuing into Pleasant Ridge and to Jim's room, she found the old ranger bent over, studying a map lying open on his desk.

"Morning, Jim."

"Morning Maggie," Jim said. This time Margaret didn't bother correcting the elderly man.

"I just met your son, George."

"You did? I am glad. He's a good boy and one I am quite pleased with. Heck I am proud of all my kids. He's a forest ranger up by Caucomgomoc Lake." And then Jim said with a grin, "And he's got some single friends, too."

Blushing, Margaret ignored Jim's suggestion about potential dates and asked, "Is he taking your truck?"

"No, he just putting a new canoe rack on it. He's knows that someday the pickup will be his. So he works on it from time to time and keeps it maintained. He's a pretty good mechanic." Happy to see his new friend, Jim passed her a cup and a box of pastry, "Here's a coffee and have a chocolate doughnut to go with it. The snack will stick to your ribs."

Munching on her only breakfast for the morning, Margaret looked at the map and asked, "You going somewhere?"

"Nope," Jim replied. "But you remember I told you about hanging the coin on my gramps' stone at the cemetery?" Margaret, with a mouth full of sugared chocolate, could only nod that she recalled the conversation.

The old man pointed to a spot on the map, "Well my Pépé's stone is right there, just down the road a ways. You might want to see it sometime."

"Why's that?" Margaret inquired after taking a sip of the hot brew.

"Because," but then Jim was interrupted by his youngest son entering the room as he broadcast. "Soon as I gas up the truck, it will be ready to go."

Then remembering that the reporter was listening, George finished with, "I mean the canoe rack is installed and I can't wait to put my canoe on it."

Changing the subject, George then asked, "Has Bella been in?"

"No. I was hoping she and the rest of 'em would be. Wanted Maggie to meet her, and Jim Jr., and Sue."

"Where's mom and Bella?"

"Your mother is babysitting Jr.'s three kids; the tykes are all sick, so I don't expect her back for a few days. Bella normally stops in before or after work, but her social work business, helping others, is keeping her busy."

"Is brother Jim working the ambulance?"

"Yes." The elder replied. "He's just started his week on."

"Ok, I'll swing by the station. Maybe I can catch him." George replied. "I've gotta head back to the woods and get on patrol. I'll stop back after my next tour."

Now more curious than ever about Jim's family, Margaret studied the Clark family picture even closer than before. Intent on the photograph the reporter didn't see the knowing smile that Jim and his son secretly exchanged.

With that George left with a, "Nice to meet you, let me know if you ever want to see the north country."

"Thank you," Margaret replied as she sat down and opened her electronic notebook to begin the day's dialog.

Staring at her notes to refresh her memory, she asked, "Yesterday you mentioned that there was a winter where you had a lot of experiences. Can you tell me about that year?"

"Yes," Jim started. "The cold weather challenges started in November, my first winter of being in the woods. Before moving to the Churchill Dam camp, I'd been assigned to be a part of a survey crew that was to establish a portion of the 200 miles of Allagash Waterway boundary line. In November we moved into the Lock Dam tender's camp, and by January we'd shifted to the Eagle Lake cabin. That year was the coldest winter on record and one that made us appreciate long johns and woodstoves."

"We'd only been in the Eagle Lake camp a few days when our routine was challenged…"

Like a dream, Jim reminisced that it had been early one morning when he and his surveying partners had arrived on the boundary line. That day's assignment had been to scribe corner posts–sections of where the line made a degree turn one way or another. The crew had finished their first post, when they heard the roar of an engine and people hollering out on the ice–nearby.

The crew of two had arisen before dawn, and stoked the wood stove to warm camp. While the kindling roared to life, Jim checked the outdoor thermometer fastened to the outside wall of the camp and saw that yet another day had been greeted by minus 20 degrees. This was the fourth in a row. By 7:30 A.M. their gear had been loaded onto a tote sled in anticipation of a full day in the woods. Before heading out, the crew took once last check of the outside temperature and discovered that the mercury showed that the outside air had risen to a warmer minus 18.

That winter the crew's primary mode of transportation was by snowmobile, which meant everything had to be towed by dogsled connected by a trailer hitch to a yellow, wide-track Tundra ski-doo. By eight A.M. the two-man team was on the line and hollers of "up a little–down a hair–set!" could be heard echoing throughout the hemlock forest, as the surveyor and the rod-man sought to adequately mark the state property line.

The team had been blazing trees for only a short

time when they heard the drone of an aircraft coming in low. The sound of the plane's engine was followed by the echoes of people shouting from the frozen surface of Big Eagle Lake. Jim and his partner rushed out of the woods and onto the wide open span of an arctic world.

Sitting on the ice was a small plane. Standing outside the craft was the pilot and his passenger shaken, but otherwise unharmed. After assuring the plane's occupants were ok the survey team learned that the aviator was from southern Maine. He and a friend had flown into Eagle Lake for a day's fishing.

Wondering what the weather might be like up north, they had called the Portland Jetport to inquire about ice and snow conditions on Big Eagle. The controller had assured the pilot that there was minimal snow cover in the north-country and they wouldn't need to install skis on their aircraft.

Flying north in sunny skies they had circled the lake and thinking they had clear space–landed on a frozen water surface that was covered with 18 inches of snow. When the plane's wheels cut through the snow's crust the plane came to a screeching halt, much like coasting into a brick wall. The aircraft stopped so short that the nose of the plane went down while the tail section came up. The propeller just cut through the snow, but not deep enough to bend or to damage the engine's blades.

After ensuring the aircraft was ok, the two winter rangers, with the aid of several volunteer fishermen, spent over two hours snowshoeing, and snowmobiling a hard-packed path until the pilot had a runway solid enough to allow take-off. By then a crowd had gathered and followed by the sounds of cheers and clapping, the plane taxied across the lake's surface, and broke through the puffs of snow stirred up by the spinning prop. Once up to speed, the aircraft rose airborne and headed to southern Maine.

Jim spent another month surveying out of the Eagle Lake camp and then was assigned to the Chamberlain Bridge camp to cover the Chamberlain and Allagash Lake District for the month of February.

That night, with the day's interview fresh on her mind, Margaret settled into the one overstuffed chair in her apartment and opened another of Jim's diaries. Once again there was a specific part of the log that stood out.

From the diary of James Clark

Box It

"Put a box on her, boys!" The man loudly announced even though he was in the deepest phase of sleep. My coworker and I had been immediately awoken by this unexpected shout from the opposite side of the camp. Outside the expansive sound of canon roared across Little Eagle Lake as subzero temperatures announced that the extreme cold had pressure ridges under construction.

My coworker, Larry, and I had been hired by the Department of Conservation to survey a portion of the 250-mile property line that delineated the state ownership of the Allagash Wilderness Waterway. We'd been working on the line for four months and due to good progress, in early February we'd moved from the Lock Dam Bangor Hydro camp to the state's one-room camp that housed the Eagle Lake ranger during the summer months.

In order to arrive at our assigned housing we'd driven a four-wheel pickup 60 odd miles northwest from Millinocket to Chamberlain Bridge. Once at the bridge we'd load up tote sleds hooked to two snowmobiles for a 25-mile trek over the ice to a one-room log cabin on Little Eagle Lake. Once on site we would work for two weeks, then the schedule allowed us two days off. During time off we'd be heading back to town and do laundry, pick up mail, pay bills and finally purchase enough groceries for the next 14 days.

At work the two of us ran a staff compass and rod, and blazed trees to mark the boundary line through the dark forest. Nights were spent under the camp's two propane lights studying the Department's property line maps. From which we'd trace lines and copy down the measurements of such compass readings as N15 degrees 42 minutes

E for a distance of 2,384 feet. After cutting and blazing, we would use a survey chain to measure each foot. Once the total distance for that section had been reached, then a corner post would be set and scribed with AWW 49. Then another reading would be set on the compass of N18 degrees 40 minutes W for a distance of 1,562 feet, at the end of which AWW Station number 48 would be established.

In this way we hopscotched through the woods sometimes accomplishing 2,500 feet a day, some days finishing 4,000 feet and other times more or less. The amount of trees marked depended on if we were swamping a path through thick underbrush where we could only see a few feet at a time, or traversing a hardwood ridge, where vistas opened and long distances sighted.

The lake was our only source of water for both drinking and washing. With outside temperatures running as much as -25 to -40 each night, it didn't take long for Little Eagle to grow thick with ice.

Our day usually began at five in the morning, Larry would begin breakfast while I would strap on snowshoes and walk 80 feet to the lake with an ice chisel and water pail, to chop a hole for water for camp.

Once back inside, I'd make our lunch so we could stay on the line until dark. Larry did the dishes and packed the maps and gear needed for the day's work. We always planned on being in the woods after sunup.

This routine was followed day after day. However, as the temperatures remained cold, the thickness of the ice grew. Every morning, in order to get camp water, I'd have to cut through another inch or two of ice, with the blue thickness eventually reaching over three feet.

Every so often the monotony of

our long days and cold nights would be broken by a stay of overnight visitors. We always enjoyed company because the comradeship interrupted the dullness of long nights and provided with news beyond range of the limited reception of the AM radio.

One of our more frequent guests was the Waterway Supervisor. Every few weeks he would arrive unannounced to check our progress and see if we needed any supplies. After supper one evening I told the seasoned woodsman that the lake ice was getting so thick that it was becoming almost impossible to cut through.

Lighting his pipe, the man thought for a moment and then in slow deliberation—offered a solution. Answering in an accent that bordered on the Maine version of a southern drawl he instructed, "Ya' kno boys, after ya cut the hole through the ice, if you place, a cardboard box over the openin', the watar won't freeze soo thick. That way in tha mornin' you won't have to do so much choppin'."

Larry and I agreed that might work, so before going to bed we placed a large corrugated box over the waterhole and after a few games of cards, we turned in for the evening. We knew that our visitor had a reputation for being quite noisy during his sleep, but that night was much worse that we'd ever imagined. After spending the nighttime with him in the cabin, I figure his wife must have worn ear plugs to get any sleep.

Laying in his bunk the man closed his eyes and immediately started the evening's rest by grinding his teeth, a sound similar to a hungry man chowing down a slice of very tough beef. Soon the chomping turned into a choking sound, like the meat had been eaten too fast and the man was in dire need of the Heimlich maneuver.

In between the chewing and choking came the snoring, snorting, coughing, gurgling, burping, and grunting and other noises beyond description.

This routine would go on for a time and then he'd be quiet for a couple of minutes, long enough for us to think he was done and we could get some sleep-only to hear him begin the routine all over. The issue of dealing with thick ice in the waterhole must have weighed heavy on his mind because in the middle of one pause he unexpectedly hollered at the top of his lungs...

"Put a box on her, boys!"

Larry and I gave up on sleep and played several games of cribbage under the quiet glow of a single L.P. gas light. Our company continued emitting a variety of sounds until early the next morning.

Closing the pages of the red hardcover Margaret realized she was beginning to understand why each entry began with a title and confirmation of the author.

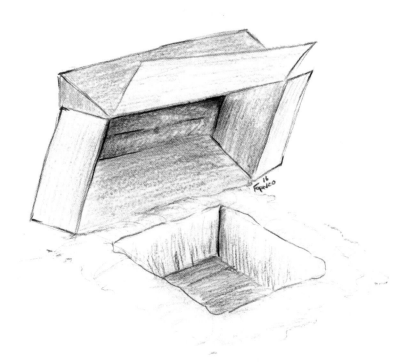

"Put A Box On Her, Boys!"
Illustration by Franklin Manzo, Jr.

Reader's Notes:

10
CHAMBERLAIN LAKE

The next morning Margaret got up early. Leaving the comfort of a warm bed, she pulled a sweater over her flannel pajamas to ward off the morning chill, and put a pot of coffee on the stove to perk. She grabbed a doughnut left over from the previous day that Jim had insisted she take. Margaret had thought about the diaries all night. Today she didn't need to hurry to Pleasant Ridge because it was Saturday and Jim was spending the day with his wife at the house of his oldest son.

Sitting at the kitchen work station, she opened another red hard-cover diary and on the first page, once again, found a heading and confirmation of who had written the journal:

From the diary of James Clark

Pressure

I had a close call today and one I'll not repeat. Guess I should have known something was gonna happen because when I walked to my ski-doo I shuddered as if someone was walking over my grave. But little did I realize how close I came to seeing judgment day.

I was snowmobiling up Chamberlain lake to ensure that someone hadn't broken down, gotten lost, or to check for any infraction of state laws. It had been a very busy weekend on the lake with tons of folks fishing and otherwise enjoying the outdoors. It seemed that smoke from warming fires rose from every cove in any out of the wind spot that could be found.

There was plenty of ice and many had added extensions onto their gasoline augers in order to drill through the four-foot, rock-hard blue thickness. And for those who wanted to fish in the middle of the lake, ice shacks had been moved into place and dotted the arctic landscape. It was a good day to be outside and folks were experiencing success.

Before I had reached the historic Chamberlain Farm, I saw that one family had experienced much success. On the ice laid several types of fish. There were brook trout of three pounds or bigger, two toque that were at least five pounds, several whitefish that were 18 inches or more in length. This is also a good time of year to catch cusk. One party had cut up chunks of a 10-pound of the ugly, but tasty, eel-like fish that many consider as tasty as a scallop.

A young boy and slightly older girl were busily cooking hot dogs, while the mom was pouring hot chocolate. Their fire had been built far enough out on the ice so it wouldn't damage the root system of the nearby shoreline.

Suddenly a flag from one of their traps sprung up and the whole family raced to see who could get to it first. I waved and left the family to their outing.

When I neared Hog Point I saw a huge fire over Ellis Brook way and so headed over. What I didn't know was that in the night a huge pressure ridge had developed between two points of land. Hog Point to the east and in the west, to no-name peninsula near Donnely Point.

Running over a mile in length, this five-foot-high, serrated wall of ice zig-zagged in front of me the width of the lake. I'd heard that these ridges were very dangerous. The thousands of pounds of ruptured pressure caused by expansion of ice would cause sheets of frozen surface to overlap into frozen peaks of ice (called sails with the icy shelves under water called keels).

The tall barrier of ice in front of was impenetrable. So I traveled paralleled to the mass and looked for a low place to cross. Motoring slowly I finally found a pass in the shield and slowly navigated between two ridges. Surveying Mother

Nature's work I was mesmerized by the sheer magnitude of the strength that had caused such upheaval.

When I crossed over the ice pass, I saw that on the other side was an opening in the frozen surface and crystal clear water was directly ahead. I was too close to the water to stop on the slippery surface, if I'd tried I would have slid into the wet brink.

With the thumb on my right hand I punched the throttle of the snowmobile to wide open. As a result, the engine accelerated to maximum RPM; the clutch engaged and the Ski-doo jumped forward.

Acting as one; the machine and I hit the open water with such force we skimmed across and sprayed the open lake surface behind me as I went.

Within seconds I was once again on solid lake, feeling very much relieved. Worried that others might follow my track, I marked the area with small fir trees from shore and flagged the danger area with orange nylon tape.

The wall of ice remained in place until spring but the open water on each side of the frozen obstruction froze solid within a couple of days. Since that day I've learned to respect all bodies of water and how quick their temperament can change.

Oh yes—the blaze. The fire I saw was a huge bonfire built by a couple of guys who decided that it was easier to chainsaw the campsite sign and picnic table than trudge into the woods for firewood. I spoke sternly to them about destruction of state property and issued invitations for them to join me in court. I am sure their penalty will be substantial.

*****

Pressure Ridges create a wall of ice, usually exposing open water on either side. Illustration by Franklin Manzo, Jr.

Sitting in his son's livingroom, surrounded by the sounds of family, Jim's mind drifted back to that first winter on Allagash Lake. It was Jim Clark's first winter as full time Allagash ranger and he felt like he'd moved into the city. Well, he hadn't actually, but some mornings it sure seemed like it; living at Chamberlain Bridge kept a ranger very busy.

Just down the road, west of the bridge and ranger's camp was a parking lot. Once the spot of the Levesque Lumber Camp, in the summer the graveled space, was used by visitors to store vehicles while canoeing downriver. In December the quiet place became a winter campground that held 50 established sites for self-contained recreational campers. Ice fishermen, snowmobilers, and explorers came and went at all hours. On a good night it wasn't unusual to hear the sound of snowmobiles and vehicles until the early hours of the next day.

But with the people came the needs of others. Broken down vehicles, snow machines, trailers, or providing information about the location of dangerously thin ice, Jim was constantly being called upon. Most of the time the winter travelers could take care of themselves and each other, but when they couldn't they came to see Jim. And with winter came alcohol, and with alcohol came trouble.

Such was the case one night when there came a loud pounding on Jim's cabin door. "A bad accident had just occurred, down the road a short way," the late night caller reported.

Upon investigation the ranger learned that a snowmobiler had drunk too much Dr. McGillicuddy's Menthol Mint Schnapps and,after feeling like the man of steel, the operator had taken his 1200 cc Renegade Enduro Ski-doo for a spin; down the middle of a nearby logging road.

But making one run wasn't enough. After completing a turn the operator decided to try a little faster ride; and headed back toward the parking lot/ campground at a speed too fast for any conditions-much less that in a crowded campground, with every shape and manner of people and vehicles all about.

In his impaired condition; he forgot about the empty trailer of a semi-logging truck parked beside the road. Luckily the driver of the sled hit the rear side tires of the trailer and glanced off. The sled was totaled, and he, well, the only good thing that can be said is, he lived. The bridge was too far from the nearest town for an immediate ambulance, so at midnight, Jim loaded the casualty onto a stretcher and into the back of a state suburban and drove the injured man to the Millinocket hospital. If the man had run into the steel frame of the trailer instead of tires, there wouldn't have been any hurry about taking the man to town, nope, no hurry at all.

A month later there was another incident regarding people drinking their favorite alcoholic beverage, only this time it happened at a nearby sporting camp, and once again–a late night call.

Reader's Notes:

11
TROUBLE IN THE MIDDLE OF NOWHERE

Deep into the night, at a time after midnight when most people are enjoying the full measure of their REM stage of sleep; the park's two-way radio blared, "Nugent's to Chamberlain Bridge. Nugent's to Chamberlain!" Stirring to conscientious from a dream of shooting Chase Rapids with his daughter Jim wondered, *Why do these calls always come in after I'm in bed?*

The previous day the ranger had rode and walked for miles in the Waterway's one-mile zone, ensuring that wood cutters complied with laws intended to protect the watershed. By 9 P.M. he had dropped into bed, physically exhausted.

The patrol had begun early and Jim had snowshoed until noon, after which he used the snowmobile to patrol north–crossed over Lock Dam and proceeded to the south end of Eagle Lake. On Lower Eagle, he spoke to several parties of fisherman, explained fishing regulations, enforced the litter law, registered campers who planned to camp overnight in a cold weather tent, and checked a party of four who were cross-country skiing the river route. At the end of each day the trekkers used hand crafted igloos for nightly accommodations, their daily direction traced by the snow and ice huts left behind.

At Smith brook, Jim had found a fresh deer killed. He'd seen a raven sitting on the ice and on investigation found a buck that coyotes had chased onto the slippery lake surface. Once on the ice, the predators had taken turns as they chased and bit through the tendons of the deer's back legs, putting it down. Jim hated to see a whitetail meet death in such a way, but realized the incident was another example of nature's *survival of the fittest* that occurred every day in the Maine woods.

Late in the afternoon Jim had returned cold and tired. After his evening tea, Jim had banked the ashes in the wood stove so the camp would hold the warmth throughout the night. He read a little about the French and Indian War exploits of Roger's Rangers, and fell into bed. He drifted off to sleep, and remembered that it would soon be school vacation and his wife and children could be with him for a whole ten days. About 1 A.M. he was awakened by the radio traffic emitting from the cabin's office.

"10-3 [go ahead], Nugent's" Jim's response flew through the airwaves to the radio located in the kitchen of the sporting camp four miles to the north.

"We've have a situation, can you come up?" The manager of the camps asked.

"10-4, I can. What's happened?"

"We've had a fight and need an ambulance; please request one from Millinocket Search and Rescue."

"Is the situation under control at this time?"

"Yes it is," the person on the other radio replied.

"10-4. What's the nature of the emergency?"

"We've got a person who's been hit in the face with a stick of firewood and the victim has received damage to one eye. He has been stabilized, but the man should see a doctor. He needs transportation by sled to the bridge, and EMTs."

"I'll be up as soon as I confirm that the medical team has been dispatched. Do we need a trooper or warden?"

"Not tonight, but one should come up in the morning. Thank you, Nugent's out."

"Chamberlain Bridge to Houlton Dispatch," Jim said using the proper language to contact the State Police Barracks in Houlton.

"Go ahead, Chamberlain," replied a radio voice so clear and professional, the radio operator could have a day job as a disc jockey.

"We have an emergency situation at Nugent's Sporting Camps on Chamberlain Lake. An individual is injured and needs evacuation to the Millinocket hospital."

"10-4 [ok], Chamberlain–standby."

"10-4." Jim replied and began putting on his cold weather gear while he waited.

"Houlton to Chamberlain Bridge," came the squawk from the two-way communication.

"Go ahead," Jim replied.

"Millinocket ambulance has been dispatched and ETA is 2:30 A.M. Is a trooper needed?"

"The situation is under control for tonight, but please be advised we will need an officer first thing in the morning."

"10-4, Jim, let me know if we can be of further help tonight. Houlton 600 out."

Jim finished putting on his snowmobile suit, facemask, and helmet, glanced at the outside thermometer and noticed the needle signified that the temperature was a hardy -20 degrees.

Jim grabbed his pack that contained a variety of emergency equipment, and with flashlight, he walked outside across crunchy snow to the winter patrol snowmobile. Before starting the machine, Jim checked to ensure that his snowshoes were firmly strapped to the sled's luggage rack.

The air was crisp, and the wood smoke from the chimney rose straight into the sky, only to turn and drifted across the face of a yellow moon. Up the lake the howl of the coyote echoed down the thoroughfare. The engine of the ranger's snowsled groaned at being started on such a cold night. However, the electric starter forced the engine to turnover and the device kicked to life. After a short warm-up, the four-cycle engine ran smoothly and Jim followed the beam of the sled's headlight out onto Chamberlain– just above where the Lake married into the frozen thoroughfare. Heading up the lake, the night was so bright he could look to his right and see most of the shoreline down into the lake's landmark known as the Arm.

Within a short time, Jim arrived at Nugent's

Camps. Established in 1936, the historic camps were well kept and the caretaker was standing on the porch of the dining hall waiting for the ranger. There were enough snowmobiles scattered about that Jim thought that each one of the half-dozen camps much be occupied.

"Come on inside. The patient is seated in the dining room and is calm for now. Have a coffee, Jim, it will be a bit before the ambulance is at the bridge and the rest of the troublemakers have either passed out or are asleep." Looking from the kitchen to the dining area, Jim saw a man sitting up stunned, but conscious, and not focused on anything in particular. Another man was sitting close to the injured person reassuring and telling him help had arrived. Someone had used first aid tape to shield the injured eye with the open end of a Styrofoam cup. Thus protected, the man could travel without causing further damage.

Inside the kitchen Jim removed his helmet and when he pulled off the face mask, he felt a burning sting on his check. The tingle, caused because his helmet's metal snap had contacted bare skin, which left him with the perfect red outline of the buckle.

"What happened?" Jim asked as he removed a notepad and pencil from his pack to take notes for the formal report and sipped the appreciated coffee.

Soon Jim heard the story of how people in two different camps had begun arguing after a night of heavy drinking. The camp operator had spoken to both cabins several times and thought he had then quiet; but then the ruckus started all over again. A man from one camp walked over to the other to continue the fight, the second man saw the first one coming so he stepped outside onto the porch. There he grabbed a stick of maple firewood, and waited. When the intruder stepped onto the deck, the occupant hit the caller in the face with the firewood . The interloper, caught by surprise, had been hit so hard that his right eye popped out of its socket and he was knocked unconscious.

The camp's operator heard the brawl, grabbed his shotgun, and ran outside and fired two rapid shots into the air. The report of the gun echoed across the lake and sobered the two men enough so they stopped fighting. First aid was provided and the injured man prepared for a ride to the ambulance.

An hour later Jim returned to the ranger's station with the injured man, met the waiting first responder transport who immediately transferred the wounded man 60-miles to the nearest hospital.

Climbing into bed, Jim set the alarm clock for the crack of dawn, the time when he expected the state police to arrive for their investigation.

Jim knew that after the state police were finished, he was scheduled to patrol to Allagash Lake; where a person never knew what they would find in the *coldest section of the Maine woods.*

*****

Jumping slightly as he felt a gentle touch on his shoulder, Jim's vision was suddenly filled with the sight of those beautiful blue eyes he loves so much.

"Time for dinner Dear.", said Susan as she offered her hand to help him from the chair he'd been napping in.

Reader's Notes:

12
THE LAKE BEYOND

Margaret had been consumed by the words she discovered in this treasure trove of tales. As soon as she finished one log book, she'd pick up another. In a short time she realized why the volumes had been so organized—*Jim had prepared a book!* That is why the first page of each entry is titled and the author identified. *Did he plan to publish his life's work, or had the information been prepared for someone else? But for whom?* She could only wonder,

From the diary of James Clark
Gob

Anyone who works with people soon learns that at some point they will be asked to respond to an emergency situation. These calls for assistance can range from forest fires, to vehicle accidents, to theft; or medical situations from minor cuts and bruises, to embedded fishhooks; or severe trauma such as broken bones, heart attacks and drowning's. A ranger needs to remain alert and prepared to act as a first responder to any call and, if necessary, arrange transport at a moment's notice.

The regimen of being outdoors in extreme weather can be physically demanding; especially for those people who may be out of shape or suffering from heart disease, diabetes, or some other ailment. Smokers or people who are overweight or have high blood pressure are often in the high risk ranks.

One way to determine if a person

is at jeopardy is to check for gray coloration of exposed skin, such as on their face and neck. Another is through conversation. If the individual is slurring their words or having difficulty with pronunciations, then they may be exhibiting early signs of a seizure or stroke.

During a routine patrol one cold winter day I ran into something totally unexpected, something I haven't seen since, someone displaying very odd behavior.

Allagash Lake is open to ice fishing only for the month of February. Because of the lake's reputation for good fisheries and the limited season, folks flock to the lake in the deepest part of winter to jig for brook trout, lake trout, and whitefish. On opening day, it isn't unusual for dozens to be on the ice.

The day started out fine, but a massive storm was predicted so, early that morning, I left by snowmobile for a cross-country trip to check parties. I arrived on the lake about 11 A.M. and there were already people scattered about. But with the approaching weather front, and temperatures dropped fast. A day that started in the comfortable 20 degree range soon turned nasty. A nor'easter was on the way with wind chills of 30 to 40 below zero—weather considered to be colder than a moose yard.

Snow was falling and the howling wind soon whipped the blizzard into a fury. I pulled onto the lake and saw two men jigging for fish several yards off the Ice Cave campsite. I pulled up, shut off my snowmobile, and surveyed the pair standing with their backs to the wind.

The fishermen were bundled in heavy parkas, wool pants, and double-knit caps pulled low over their heads. It was so cold that the snow had frozen to the men's eyebrows and icicles hung off frozen beards.

In the wailing wind I inquired "Cold, ain't it?" The response from one of the men was a garbled "mi arms r oze." Not understanding what the man said, I said, "I can't understand, what you are saying?"

Once again the man said louder, "mi arms r oze." Worried that I might be witnessing a person having a stroke, I asked again, "What? talk, slower!"

"With that the man spit a brown gob into his mitted hand and pronounced with clarity, "My worms are froze."

"Guess they are ready to use now though," I replied and made a mental note to stick to lures when fishing in winter temperatures.

Unknown fisherman Allagash Lake February 1989.
Tim Caverly photograph

Absorbed by the information, Margaret read
another account:

From the diary of James Clark

Cold Room

When you're a ranger who works in the woods, it's necessary to work closely with other agencies. In fact, for safety, it is extremely important to cooperate.

One February day a game warden friend, Brian came to camp and asked "I have to check beaver trapper sets today and the snow is so deep, I am worried about my snowmobile getting stuck or breaking down. Can you get away?"

Brian is a big man, with a sense of humor that matches his size. He'd worked for a while as an Allagash Ranger, during the formative years of the park. He was a dedicated outdoorsman and had trapped, guided, and sometimes worked as a woods operator. I'd never seen the man get into a situation he couldn't get out of; so I suspected he wanted company more than he was worried about breaking down. Brian had helped me on a number of occasions, and I always learned something whenever we were together. I had caught up with my project list, and it never hurt to make one more check of the lake, so I agreed to go.

We traveled 18-miles up Chamberlain, and left the lake at the Upper Crow's Nest campsite. From there we motored across to Otter Pond to check a trapper's muskrat and beaver sets. Finding the sets legal, my warden friend, Brian, suggested that we stop into a local sporting camp, Loon Lodge on Round Pond in T7R14.

Now, Loon Lodge is at the south edge of the Carry Trail of the portage trail from Round Pond, and are located at an historic canoe route. For years summer travelers paddled north on Caucomgomoc Lake, waded and poled up Ciss Stream, and once at Round Pond, carried the three miles across to Allagash Lake. Today, the sporting camp is still a very popular spring, summer and fall destination.

For a short period the owner of Loon Lodge hired a local fur trapper to open the camps during the February fishing season. The caretaker tended traps during the day, and then at night cared for the sportsmen that fished the artic lake. Brian wanted to visit the Lodge, to make sure everything was ok with the caretaker and the clients.

Arriving in the camp yard, we shut off our sleds just as our friend, Ben, opened the kitchen door of the cook camp and invited, "Coffee is ready!"

The day had been very cold, and we were wet from spending hours in blowing snow. So the idea of something hot and a chance to dry off felt welcome.

After a few minutes of standing beside a glowing woodstove, and discussing the events of recent days, the trapper asked, "Have you ever been in the camps before?" When I replied that I hadn't, the custodian offered to show me around. Leaving the warm kitchen, we entered an elaborate living room with a roaring fireplace. A trophy area whose walls bragged with mounts of deer; moose antlers and several plaques of a large speckled square tails; the adornment finished nicely by a bear skin rug.

Passing through the room designed for conversation and tall tales, we proceeded up a set of stairs leading to the second story. Opening the door of the master bedroom, our friend proudly announced, "This is my room."

I walked into the spacious bedchamber and, even though it was bitterly cold outside, I noticed the north facing window was wide open. Without hesitation, I stated, "Jeepers, Ben, your room's cold!"

"Yeah," he replied. Ben then reached under the double bed and pulled out a brown carcass and proclaimed, "it keeps my beaver froze!"

Another lesson learned, if I ever start trapping I'll know where to keep my critters until I am ready to skin and process the fur.

*****

After a wonderful day with his family, Jim returned to his room at Pleasent Ridge. Alone with his thoughts, his mind was soon drifting back to the north Maine woods...

*****

Too soon the morning after the fight a trooper knocked on the ranger's door. Fortunately, the policeman had brought a sled with him, and so after a brief debriefing about the nights before, Jim escorted him to Nugent's Camps. Jim checked with the officer to ensure he was all set because he still planned to go to Allagash Lake. The trooper had nodded, and said, "That's fine, and you've provided me with all of the information I need. From what you've told me, I'll contact the injured party to see if he wants to make a formal complaint, and if he does, I'll make an arrest. In any event both parties will be summoned for their part of the disturbance."

Heading northwest on Chamberlain, Jim passed

by a number of winter users engaged in a variety of winter activities. There were fishermen jigging for whitefish off the mouth of Leadbetter Stream, a group of sleds left the Farm Camps crossing the lake southwest where they would drive across Mud Pond Carry and continue to Chescuncook Village. At the Village the sledders bought gasoline and ordered a hot lunch, and rented a room at the well-known tourist destination the Chescuncook House. When Jim neared historic Lock Dam, he saw another group of fisherman fishing close to shore for squaretails. Farther to the north of McCarran Point, another group of snowmobiles were just pulling into Tramway Cove on their way across 3,000 feet of land to the trains abandoned beside Eagle Lake.

The last party Jim saw on the lake were fishing near the old railroad trestle, at the mouth of Allagash Stream, but still in an area where motorized vehicles were allowed. Regardless, Jim checked the upstream side of the old locomotive crossing for any sign of snowmobile tracks, and not finding any headed to the Upper Crow's Nest campsite and to the Ledge Road. Once on the woods road owned by Seven Island Lumber Company, he would follow the unplowed road until he turned north onto a packed trail leading to the Island campsite on Allagash Lake.

Arriving at the campsite, Jim was pleased to see the snowmobiles of today's visitors; parked above the high water mark, obeying the Waterway regulation that prohibited the year round use of combustible engines on the water, except by law enforcement officials.

Driving out onto the lake, Jim's first stop was at a fisherman who was using worms to catch a brook trout by the first island on the lake. Jim pulled up just in time to see the man bring up a 16-inch squaretail through the hole.

"Nice fish, how much ice is there?" the ranger asked.

"Three feet and its damn hard ice too! Don't make no sense I can't bring my gasoline ice auger out here. Do you know how long it takes to chisel through 36 inches of diamond-hard ice?" the fisherman said as he put another worm on his hook and dropped the line back through the hole in the ice.

Before Jim could answer the man got another hit. "Holy, this is a big one, bet it's a granddaddy—he-he." the man shouted in glee. Just then Jim noticed a bunch of people fishing down by the outlet of the lake, and so he wished the man "Good luck" and started his snowmobile to head over.

Pulling up to a group about 65 yards off the lake's outlet, Jim spoke to each one. He reminded one fisherman eating shrimp, who threw a piece of the red delicacy into the jig hole, that the fishing regulations required the use of artificial lures or worms only, and baiting was prohibited. Otherwise, everyone was enjoying a day outside.

Putting on the snowshoes he always carried, Jim walked through the woods to the outlet of Otter Pond, where he found four planes on skis waiting for their pilots and passengers to return from Allagash Lake. Returning from the small flowage, Jim was pleased to find the remains of one of Al Nugent's (the 1936 founder of Nugent's Camps) line camps. These were small log shelters, that some considered nothing more than a trap line hovel, just big enough for one man to escape the cold. Each shack had been constructed within a day's travel of each other so Nuge could be assured of protective cover from frozen elements when he snow-shoed and skied a two-week trek, a distance of 75 miles, to check beaver, bobcat, muskrat, and fisher sets.

Picture of Al Nugent from the Rob and Stella Flewelling Collection

The hut, despite the building's age, still seemed habitable. *It must have been a relief, after covering the 10 miles from the last camp near Chamberlain, to arrive at this outpost; build a fire, escape the minus temperature wind chills; and dry his wet clothing before heading out at the next crack of dawn.* Jim thought. The ranger then sat on an exposed section of a near-by fir blowdown, removed the thermos from his day pack and poured a cup of hot ice tea. Comfortable, the woodsman stared at the structure and let his imagination create a mental image. *I can see old Nuge now stomping through 12 inches of fresh snow as he arrived late in the day and when it was getting too dark to see. Using an old rusted shovel left hanging on the side of the building, he'd clear the snow away from the door. The structure, solidly built from standing rounded logs nailed side by side, measured 8 feet x 10 feet and was big enough for one person and their gear.*

On the southeast side of the building stood a 24-inch-wide x 66-inch-tall door. This location ensured that an open entrance could capture any warmth offered by a morning sun. The exterior panels of the door were covered with sheets of birch bark so that somebody with a flashlight after dark could easily pick up the brightness of the entrance. Hinges for the door were nothing more than cutout pieces of leather straps. The doorknob was one stick horizontally nailed midway up the door, that when closed, would ride up over another that stuck out perpendicular from the frame. By sliding one stick over the other, entrance to the building could be gained, or by pulling a small rope on the inside, the door could be closed.

Windows on the east and west side of the building offered light to the inside. The roof had pole trusses over which cedar shakes had been fastened to seal the shelter from the weather. A six-inch, metal stovepipe stuck through the north side of the roof proved there would be an opportunity to have a warming fire inside. A long and narrow cabinet nailed along the exterior of the east wall provided a chance to store cold supplies or, more importantly, trapping scent, outside.

Inside the building, Jim imagined a single room designed for convenience and one that utilized all available space. A nail on the south wall near the door would hold a pair of snowshoes. The floor was built of split logs with the flat side up. Along the north wall there would have been a cutout in the floor that measured about 30 inches x 42 inches, in which a small woodstove served a dual purpose of providing heat and cooking. Along the east side of the interior sat a sturdy spruce pole bunk laced with fresh balsam fir boughs. The 30-inch wide by 80-inch long bed was high enough off the floor to store pack baskets, fire wood, and other goods, was just wide enough to sleep one person comfortably on the fragrant mattress. On the opposite was waited a rough sawn table, and a homemade birch chair.

Al Nugent's snowshoes.
From the collection of the Robin Holyoke Family

Once inside, the voyager opened the door of the small woodstove and with nearly frozen limbs, struck a match to light the kindling laid up from the last visit. Nuge's fingers were so stiff with cold that it would take several tries before he could get the wooden match to strike. Once he heard the snap of the cedar *kindling announce that the fire had caught, Al would add two or three pieces of dry hardwood onto the softwood igniter. With a fire burning, he'd then reach for a couple of candles waiting on a nearby shelf. The wax torches served as his illumination for the evening.*

Within a matter of minutes the camp would be a body-thawing 75 degrees. The trapper would remove the wide leather belt that held his holstered Colt 45 Bisley Hunter Long 1871 patent model handgun he always carried—just in case he ran into a bad varmint—and it didn't matter if the polecat was four legged or two legged. Once unstrapped, he'd hang the revolver on a wooden peg within reach and strip down to his inside clothing of a one-piece red Union suit with the drop seat in the back, knit wool stockings, moccasins and felt hat. Comfortable, he'd boil water, add dried vegetables, and cook up a hot meal of muskrat stew or boiled beaver.

Al Nugent's Colt 45 Bisley Hunter Revolver
From the collection of the Robin Holyoke family.

While the meat cooked, Nuge would take a tin
coffee can, by the container's handmade [telephone]

wire bale, fill the tea pail with snow, and place the frozen water on the stove to melt and steep for tea. Once the beverage was hot, Al would add a dried *beaver castor for the health of it.

After supper he'd likely rough skin and flesh the pelt of any critter he'd picked up from nearby Otter Stream, roll the bobcat, muskrat, beaver, for fisher pelts in preparation of further stretching and drying the skins once back at his main camp.

The next morning the trapper would throw off a rough wool blanket and rise before the sun. Al would get dressed in a camp without heat, because the fire had gone out during the night. He'd make a lunch of either chilled boiled beaver or peanut butter and bacon sandwich (because peanut butter and bacon won't freeze in arctic temperatures) and pack his tea pail to cook a hot drink for his noon meal. The last chore before heading to the next series of sets and another camp; would be to prepare a startin' fire in the wood stove. He'd lay a wad of birch bark on top of cold ashes, and on top of the tinder, Nuge would add

---

*Author's note: A beaver caster is the scent gland from a beaver; and every beaver has two. The 'caster' has a multitude of uses: to make scent for trapping; an ingredient in woman's perfume, a natural food additive to increase the tasete of such flavors as raspberry and strawberry, and for use as a natural health supplement. According to trappers, dried castors added to one's drink lowers blood pressure, calms heart rate, and eases stress.

a bundle of split cedar kindling, just in case the next time he'd arrived wet, nearly frozen, and someone who needed a fire in a hurry.

By the time Nuge had covered the complete trotline and returned to his Chamberlain Lake camp, he likely would have a pack of fur skins weighing well over 100 lbs.

A light breeze knocked a clump of snow from an overhead spruce limb, and down the neck of Jim's winter jacket–a chilling coldness that returned the man to today's world.

Sounds romantic, but must have been damn hard way to make a living, Jim thought as he returned the thermos into the pack, stood and headed towards his sled and his patrol route.

It was early afternoon by the time the ranger returned to his snowmobile left by the glacial ledges, near the inlet to Lower Allagash Stream. After tying the snowshoes onto the tracked vehicle, Jim started the machine and headed toward a scheduled meeting with a land company forester. They'd made the appointment to review an application to remove spruce, fir, hemlock and cedar conifers within the Waterway's one-mile harvesting zone.

Supervisor Tim Caverly inspecting a cutting operation south of Allagash
Stream T7R13
From the Tim Caverly Collection

Jim choked the sled once and the machine
started easily. Pulling on his face mask and helmet,
Jim noticed large white flakes from an unpredicted
snowstorm had begun to fall and that a northeast wind
was building fast. The pilots fishing by the Outlet
campsite sensed the approaching storm, and pulled
up their ice fishing traps and headed to their planes
waiting nearby. It was time to fly out while they still
could and maybe, just maybe, they could dodge the
storm and make it home.

Reader's Notes:

13
FROZEN

From the diary of James Clark
Discombobulated

I am not sure that I should record this incident, and can't believe the episode really happened. Frankly—I am really quite uncomfortable talking about it. But in the essence of showing how quickly even the simplest acts can go haywire in the wilderness, it is with reluctance that I leave this as a record for others☹

The occasion began innocently enough. I had arrived one evening to visit with two game warden friends, Brian and Alvin. It was late February, and they were housed in a rustic log accommodation. The building, built in the 1940s located on the bank of Chamberlain Thoroughfare, was warm and dry. Even during the winter cold, it was a living space so snug that field mice would move inside to share the luxury of being indoors, despite the human occupants.

Outside birds and squirrels frequented nearby feeders and every once in a while a white-coated ermine would burst from under the porch to invite an unsuspecting red squirrel back under the building for lunch.

I had joined the two for an evening visit in preparation for an early start to the next day. Their role on the morrow was to arise before sun-up to check the Chamberlain District for any ice fishing traps left unattended. [State law required that ice fishing sets be checked at least once every hour.] We had a pleasant evening of sharing tales about the old days and discussing, lore, legends and mysteries only found in the forest. The two even showed me a secret 'cache' under the sink.

For years, they explained, the warden's cabin had housed officers assigned to the Chamberlain District. But the building also served as a staging area for those from downstate in the area on 'temporary duty.' While the inhabitant kept a supply of their favorite medicinal drink for personal use, it was sometimes necessary to put the liquor out of sight from visitors that got too relaxed.

As is customary around many tables; before supper a proper host will offer an unexpected overnight guest a 'hummer' from their therapeutic stock. The beverage served over ice with hors d'oeuvres, ensures that the visitor will gently slide into a state of relaxation. But sometimes, temporary company will imbibe a little too much and it becomes necessary for the full time occupants to hide their libations. Such was the case at the Chamberlain Thoroughfare camp.

Along the front of the kitchen cabinet is a door that provides access to the area directly under the counter and to the sink's plumbing. Upon examination underneath the S-trap, on the cabinet's floor, an inquisitive person will find a loose board. Under the easily removed plank, there is a secret compartment big enough to house a jug of the resident's favorite nourishment —often labeled 'Old Crow.'

So on this particular evening, they exposed the hidden store. Lifting the board, there was a transparent green but empty, bottle of 'Davis's Pain Killer.' A medicine created in the middle of the 19th century, the label on the flask proudly announced that the vegetable elixir contained 51% ethyl alcohol and opiates—and "that the elixir was good for man or beast." The decanter, while empty and obviously planted as a treasure to discover, brought to mind even more late night tales. Finally with a "let's do this again sometime" we hit the hay.

The next morning, I'd planned to meet with a landowner representative to discuss a recent timber trespass onto public land. Two days before, the forester had called to explain, "an anxious jobber had driven their skidder across the state's boundary line, and illegally removed several large pumpkin pines. The conifers were very valuable and a prize too tempting to resist." So it was my role, as ranger, to determine the scope of the violation and settle a resolution with the landowner.

At 3 A.M, the wardens rose to prepare for their day's work. Unable to sleep, I got up as well to and enjoyed morning coffee with my friends. After they'd 'hit the trail' I packed a lunch and thermos of hot tea; because I expected to be on snowshoes most of the day.

By four O'clock, although the sun was not yet up, I was wide awake and so decided to drive my four by four to the location of the violation about 25-miles to the north. It was there that the forester and I were to cruise and tally the damage.

Driving down a woods road that had been scraped rather than sanded, I watched the banks of the icy way for any sign of deer, moose, coyotes, or partridge budding in a yellow birch. After 45 minutes, the night still claimed dominion over the day. I contemplated a cup of the heated liquid. Not wanting to stop the truck, or turn on a light I rationed "I can pour the tea into my cup, surely I'll know when the cup is full."

Placing the thermos between my legs, I unscrewed the chrome cup and removed the stopper. Slowing the vehicle to a crawl, in order to prevent spillage, I deliberately poured the steaming tea into the cup resting on the top of my left foreleg. Suddenly the vehicle's right tire lurched into and bounced out of a pothole. This pitch caused the tea to overflow the unbreakable mug. The boiling heat soaked through my wool pants, long johns, and seared the skin of my leg underneath.

My clothes, worn to keep out the cold also held in the heat of the scorching liquid. I could feel blisters from the 2nd degree burn building. Wanting to relieve the pain, I bailed out of my truck, pulled down my two layers of pants, and packed snow on the damaged skin to cool the scald as quickly as possible.

I exited the vehicle so quickly that I'd forgotten to take my truck out of gear. So I am standing on the edge of a plowed road, with my pants down to my knees, watching my truck go down the road without a driver.

Hobbled, and not wanting to scrape my pants up over the singed skin,

I shuffled down the road, and only caught up with the truck when the left front tire of the 4x4 stuck in a snow bank.

After shutting off the vehicle, I stayed there another ten minutes applying snow to the burn. Luckily no one discovered my predicament and this is the first time I've mentioned it to anyone.

However, due to the severity of the damage to the skin, I carried a sizeable scar for several weeks. While others did not know of my accident, my four-year-old daughter wasn't much help. Whenever I would wear shorts around the house, she would point at the four by three inch scar and shout in a little girl voice to whoever would listen "Daddy's got a bad boo-boo!"

Out of curiosity, Margaret turned the page to skim the next entry. Reading the heading, the inquisitive reporter was drawn to read further.

From the diary of James Clark
Lost in a Whiteout

Well diary, There was another instance last night that ended up ok, but could have led to a much different conclusion.

I had gone to bed and had just begun to drift off into dreamland when my sleep was suddenly interrupted.

About 10 P.M. a snowmobile pulled up beside the camp and someone pounded on my front door. From outside came a frantic hollering, "Ranger, Ranger! Jim, Jim, are you in there? For god's sake Jim, are you there?"

After lighting a propane gas light to let the caller know I was up; I opened the door. In a steamy swirl, the warm air of my cabin immediately confronted the extreme cold from the outside. On the porch stood a visitor completely hidden by a helmet, face mask, and snowmobile suit. The man entered through the escaping steam and removed his head gear. "What's the matter?" I inquired.

The caller quickly declared, "My friend is lost. I can't find him anywhere! Can you help?" While I listened, the man explained "my buddy and I were returning from visiting the Farm Camps, when suddenly he throttled his snowmobile to full speed and sped away. I watched his red taillight disappear in a swirling cloud of snowy white.

"The trail was rough and I figured that he was cold and in a hurry to get back to the warmth of our camper in the parking lot, so I just tootled along at normal speed.

"But when I returned, our trailer was dark and my friend wasn't anywhere to be seen. So I went back out to the lake, but the wind is blowing so hard I couldn't see a thing. Have you seen him?"

Before I could answer, the man said in a trembling voice, "I am afraid he is either lost or maybe even drove into the open water of the nearby Chamberlain Bridge thoroughfare."

I instructed the guest to "return to his camper, and make coffee for when his partner returned. And that "I'd get dressed and go out for a look."

The sledder offered to go with me but I told him it would be better if he waited at his camp. The frantic man looked cold, tired, and nervous. I didn't need to worry about rescuing two people.

By 11:00 P.M. I was on my sled heading out the trail en route for Chamberlain. Once at the lake, I swung toward the open water of the Chamberlain thoroughfare. But I didn't find any tracks, so I was fairly certain the man hadn't traveled that way.

I swung north and drove headlong into a northwest wind. The gusts were blowing so hard that the snow was swirling around like little whirlwinds. Encased by a complete whiteout, it was impossible for me to see more than a few feet in any direction. I felt as if wrapped up in a frozen blanket.

On a hunch, under the illumination of my sled's headlight, I took a compass reading and headed to where I hoped I'd hit the south edge of the Arm of Chamberlain. I lucked out and found the shore near where the Arm leaves the main lake.

Keeping the shoreline off my right shoulder I headed down the three miles section to the end of the long and narrow cove. Moving slowly, I watched for any sign of movement or a headlight. Nearing the end, the whiteout cleared just long enough to see a beam appear and then immediately disappear. Drawing closer, the headlamp materialized, and then vanished. By now I had marked his location.

At the very end of the Lake's extension, I came upon our friend with his snowmobile stuck to the floorboards. He was standing in the middle of a 50-foot-long dip of slush. The snowy mush appeared to be ten inches deep, and had been disguised by 12 inches of fresh powder.

I parked my sled well away from the water-laden snow and approached the individual. Walking up I could smell the strong scent of burning rubber from the neoprene belt of an overworked snowmobile clutch.

The stranded man explained that he'd left his friend to play a trick, but got lost in the whiteout and accidently drove into the arm. When he'd tried to turn around, the snowmobile got buried in the large pocket of slush. The track of his sled was packed with so much of the heavy icy mush that the Ski-doo had become as heavy like deadweight.

Frightened, he'd spent the last

two hours trying to break his ski-
doo free from its involuntary prison.
Exhausted, the stranded snowmobiler
was dehydrated, exhausted, and chilled
to the bone.

In an effort to get him moving and
warmed up, I grabbed my ax and we
walked to shore. Out of the wind, we cut
down three 9-foot long fir trees. Once
on the wood was on ground, we carried
the four-inch diameter logs to his sled.
Back on the ice, we cut two of the logs
into three foot sections. The third, used
as a block and pry, was placed under
the sled's trailer hitch, and we lifted the
back of his sled off the ground. Once in
the air, I had him start his sled to clear
the suspension of the frozen slurry.

Once the undercarriage had cleared,
and while I kept the rear end suspended
off the snow, he placed the remaining
sections of logs perpendicular on the
snow under the rubber track. After we
had a solid base, I released the pry and

set the sled back onto the raised wooden bed.

I then cut the pry bar into four pieces and placed two short sections of logs sideways under each ski. Then I instructed him to start my sled, and, if I could get his sled moving, he was to follow closely, and not stop.

I started his snowmobile, and once the engine was up to speed, I gave the vehicle half throttle and the sled flew off the wooden platform. By the time the vehicle hit the cold mire, the machine had gained enough momentum to carry the Ski-doo through a six-foot long stretch of mush. Still not out of the dilemma, I felt the vehicle bog down. But suddenly the equipment caught a solid surface and as one, the snowmobile and I flew onto a previously packed snowmobile track.

Once at the main lake, we swapped sleds and he followed the three miles back to the campground. His friend came to the camper door as soon as we pulled up, greatly relieved.

Oh yes! It appears that we'd arrived just in time because the man's sled ran out of gas by the front door.

Well this one turned out ok. Wonder what's going to happen tomorrow? But whatever occurs, I hope it turns out as well as last night.

Reader's Notes:

14
HEALING

The next day still feeling tired from the previous short night, Jim rode north and parallel to the east shore of the lake; the ranger thought the weather was perfect for families to enjoy the weekend outdoors. The storm of the previous night had run its course and now a light clearing wind drifted in from the northwest.

The morning sun had warmed the day and folks on bright colored snowmobiles were out and about. The chainsaw sound of augers echoed from Telos to the Trestle as the motorized drills bored holes through four feet of blue ice; a sound that revealed favorite fishing spots. The cloudless sky was a vibrant indigo and the tall evergreens that dotted the hillsides were an effervescent green.

Ice shacks were occupied and white smoke, like

a soft vapor, rose from the chimney of each shelter on the ice. Kids laughed and dogs barked as they accompanied their parents. They scooped the slush from each fishing hole, knowing a squaretail, lake trout, whitefish, or cusk could appear at any moment.

On shore, in the shadow of a large pine, a hungry red fox sat, watched, and waited for any scrap of food or fish innards dropped in the snow. Three trees over from the fox, sat a ruffed grouse on a hardwood branch, out of reach of the predator; snipping off the spring buds of a yellow birch. Behind the partridge and well up-wind of the fox hopped a snowshoe hair, larger than a rabbit, the hair's winter snow-white pelt molting into a coloration of brown and white patches. The animal's nose wiggled and kept it's ears alert for sign of danger.

Jim had gotten up before dawn and packed everything needed to be on snowmobile patrol, if necessary, until dark. The first incident happened when a day fisherman had driven his sled three miles from the parking lot at Chamberlain Bridge to Telos Lake; only to run out of gasoline. When Jim neared on his long track Skantic, the man had flagged the ranger and explained he was stranded. So Jim went back to the state's garage and then delivered three gallons of fuel to get the man home.

The ranger covered the distance from Round Pond to Telos Dam and then returned to the trail from the parking lot to Chamberlain Lake. And there were people everywhere, even at the far-east end of the Arm, where folks had set fishing sets by McNally Brook, not realizing that nearby a jet engine sat, silent in the reforested woods.

*Years before the turbine had been part of an F89c-Scorpion Fighter on a local engineering test flight from the 57th Fighter Interceptor Squadron at the Presque Isle Air Force Base. The Interceptor, piloted by Captain Vern Burke with radar observer Lieutenant Leroy Vestal, experienced a series of electrical and instrument failures on May 24, 1954.

More problems developed when the compass instruments displayed a heading error. While Burke thought they were flying north, the jet was actually heading south, 180 degrees in the wrong direction. The crew remained unsure of their location until they saw Mount Katahdin peek through the clouds. The two airmen ejected over the dike southwest of Millinocket Lake. Theirs was the first successful double ejection from an F-89.

The pilotless plane continued to fly until it

ran out of gas and crashed 65 miles north— near the Arm—not far from Telos Road mile maker number 52. Hitting ground, the plane broke up along a 300-foot glide path through the trees and was discovered 11 days later.

In the meantime, according to legend, Al Nugent had gotten to the aircraft before the military recovery team. Nuge stood near a piece of one of the wings and with compass in hand, said to his companion "if the aircraft had gone down 2 more degrees to the northwest, the plane would have landed right in the middle of my yard."

Not wanting anything to go to waste Nuge salvaged one of the jet's fuel tanks to use at a float. He'd then gone back for the plane's turbine. The woodsman dragged the jet engine northwest along an old tote road, as far as McNally Brook, that is until the Air Force arrived. The aluminum apparatus still sits deserted in the woods, where Al, and the Air Force left it many years ago.

*****

For more information about the "Engine in the Arm" see: http://www.mewreckchasers.com/f-89c.html

Continuing his patrol along the east shore of the main lake, Jim passed Nugent's main camps where *Buckshot Pete had visited with a shotgun many years before. Jim passed Gull Rock and noticed an opening in the ice where a cinnamon-colored otter had exited a plunge hole to run, slid, and play in the snow on its way to Leadbetter Stream, *where the furbearer will no doubt socialize with other semi-aquatic weasels and have a nice feed of fish*, Jim grinned. When Jim got to the stream, he slowed the throttle speed of the sled and looked for any sign of other slinky creatures in the area where Leadbetter Brook flowed into Chamberlain.

A while back he'd discovered an old trapper's diary that chronicled a log cabin which at one time had been situated on a knoll about 150 feet up the brook. The camp had been the home of trapper David Hanna, a former manager of the Chamberlain Farm for the Lincoln Pulp Wood Company.

The same journal recorded that years ago ice fisherman would sometimes jig eight whitefish an hour in a spot on the lake 100 yards off the mouth of Leadbetter. *Too bad*, he thought, *fishing isn't that good here these days*.

Two miles further Jim noted the now forested

lot where the old Heart O' Maine Sporting Camps (Harold Whiteneck–proprietor) once stood. The vacant spot had filled in nicely with pumpkin pine seedlings and small white birch.

Deciding to have a cup of hot tea, to warm up, Jim pulled up beside the nearby steel remains of the steam side-wheeler H.W. Marsh; a piece of logging history southeast of Hog Point. Shutting off his sled, Jim removed his helmet, poured tea, and contemplated all he'd heard about this piece of logging memorabilia.

* Author's Note: For the complete story of Buckshot Pete's visit to Nugent's camps see Tim Caverly's book Allagash Tails Volume IV Wilderness Ranger's Journal: Rendezvous at Devil's Elbow

Remnants of H.W. Marsh on shore at Chamberlain Farm April 2015
Photograph from Tim Caverly Collection.

The old boat, discarded years before, stood as
a final reminder of the activity that once buzzed at the
600-acre Chamberlain Farm when millions of cords
of trees floated downstream to markets as far away as
Bangor.

The boat built by O.A. Harkness, the
Admiral of the Great Northern Navy in 1903, was
manufactured on the north side of a strip of land
called the Tramway, near the shore of Eagle Lake
in unorganized township T7R12. The vessel 91-feet
long, had a 25-foot beam, 2 vertical wood burning

boilers, and drew 4 feet of water. Once launched, the transport spent five years booming logs down Eagle Lake to the endless conveyor.

Once delivered to the Tramway, the timber would be loaded onto the steel cable conveyance, and moved 3,000 feet over land where the tree length logs were dumped into Chamberlain Lake. It is estimated that during the six years of the Tramway's operation, 100 million feet of long logs rode the rail over the divide.

After the Marsh's job was finished on Eagle, the craft was moved to Chamberlain to accompany the towboat George A. Dugan. The two ships worked about 10 years tugging log booms 24 miles southeast to Telos Dam and the East Branch of the Penobscot River. When the transports weren't working, the vessels were docked at Chamberlain Farm.

The assignments for the Marsh effectively ended one fall after the boat partially froze into the ice of Chamberlain Lake. In order to protect the engine; the stern was cut off just behind the paddle box and the front pulled up on shore. When the ice went out in the spring thaw, the stern floated away.

Jim thought, *I should reread the books*, The Wilderness Farm by Dr. Dean Bennett and The

Allagash by Legendary Maine Guide Gil Gilpatrick *to reacquaint with that part of Maine's logging history.*

Leaving the farm behind Jim traveled to Lock Dam where he spoke with two parties who had been on the ice most of the day. Jim was pleased when he checked a family of four who had been very successful. A boy and girl proudly pointed at their catch, whitefish arranged according to size and packed in ice and snow from nature's fresh fish market. The whitefish reminded the ranger of another local legend.

In the 1950s so many whitefish had spawn in Lock Dam Stream during their October run, that Al Nugent had dipped burlap bags full for Patty Nugent to serve as a delicacy to their guests. Any whitefish not eaten were buried in the camp's vegetable garden to fertilize the soil.

From Lock Dam, Jim continued snowmobiling north beyond McCarren Point. He was surprised that there wasn't anyone fishing in the usually popular hole. Swinging into Tramway Cove he crossed over land toward the deserted locomotives near Eagle Lake. Pulling up to the trains, the ranger estimated that there were over 50 snowmobiles parked around the two engines. Dressed in cold weather gear were men, women, and children in many activities. Several were taking pictures, some were cooking hotdogs over an open fire, and others were discussing the history of the area. When they recognized Jim, many surrounded the ranger and asked, "Whose trains were they? Is it true they were brought down the lake on the ice? Did the trains run on coal? How did the Tramway work? Why were the trains sitting so level, did someone jack them up?"

Jim had just started to interpret the area when he saw a person remove a piece from the bigger locomotive and place the artifact into a carry bag. At Jim's reproach, the man sheepishly admitted to taking an oil cover for a souvenir and handed the relic to the ranger. Jim took the object and made a mental note to permanently reattach the historical part during warmer weather.

To stress the seriousness of the man's act, the ranger then issued him a warning for removing state property. With the notice, the ranger emphasized to the visitor and everyone watching that artifacts were for the enjoyment of all, not to become part of a private collection.

Once he answered each question, Jim returned to his patrol. Turning the sled he headed back to Chamberlain Lake. Jim had to pull off to the side of the trail several times to allow sledders to pass as they headed for the trains.

Back on Chamberlain, Jim decided to check the state's nearby boundary line for any sign of maintenance such as removing blow downs or repainting of blazes. He pulled up to the tree line on the northwest side of Tramway Cove, shut off his sled, and strapped on his snowshoes and headed into the woods. Jim had traveled over a mile checking the orange painted blazed line when suddenly the whole world dropped right out from underneath him.

From the diary of James Clark
Reclaimed

Finally back at camp and what a day! Patrolling the lake I spoke to several parties, saw lots of nice trout, and even chased a coyote away from a deer splayed on the ice.

On the northwest side of Tramway Cove I snowshoed into the woods to check the condition of the boundary line in preparation of the harvest operation scheduled. Walking the line, I saw several tracks of bobcat, rabbit, and moose and even found a spruce grouse walking around.

I hadn't gone very far when I sensed a presence. I turned and saw a lynx standing in my tracks, staring at me from about 100 feet away. The big cat shadowed me all the time I was in the woods. I was on the line for three hours and the predator was there every time I turned, curious about what I was doing.

Completing my inspection, I headed

south, to the lake and my snowmobile.
Partway out I walked over a small knoll
when suddenly the ground collapsed,
and I sank to my waist in snow.

Unknowing, I had walked over
a pile of crisscrossed brush pile—once
on top—the heap collapsed. I ended
up suspended in air. My snowshoes,
under the brush, prevented me from
climbing out. I couldn't move up or
down. Eventually I managed to break
enough of the rotted branches around me
so I could reach down and remove my
snowshoes, one at a time. Once off, I was
able to pull the shoes out of the hole, roll
onto my back, and down the knoll.

At first I thought I'd fallen into a
bear's den. But I didn't stick around to
find out, and I never saw a bear. But I
did think I heard the baby-like sound of
bear cubs crying as I moved away.

Unfortunately, I had broken the
bow on my right snowshoe, which made
the implement useless. For a bit I tried

to walk wearing only one snowshoe,
but with one foot on top of the snow
and the other sinking over two feet with
every step, I soon tired. So I removed the
good shoe and waded through the snow.
I ended up trudging for over a mile
through the seemingly bottom-less cover.
By the time I arrived at my sled, I was
exhausted and soaking wet with sweat,
thankful that I didn't have farther to
travel.

Back at camp, I thought about all
I saw today and reminisced about how
the Allagash Wilderness Waterway has
recovered since the days of clear cutting,
dam building, road construction, and
endless development; all in man's
constant efforts to tame the wild.

When one studies early maps,
books, photographs, journals, and
diaries people can grasp just how many
man-made structures once dotted the
landscape. Compare the amount of
buildings, numbers of people, with the

intensity of cutting and it's a wonder that the corridor is the world class natural experience treasured today.

In the 1940s and 50s one resident, wrote about the destruction that had occurred, '"before lumbering, old timers said a person could throw an axe over his shoulder and walk through the woods anywhere, whenever he wanted. Then cutting crews arrived and millions and millions of wood that once canopied the forest, were hauled, and floated away. In areas adjacent to the Tramway, railroad, and roads, [transportation routes] forests were cut so hard that regeneration slowed to hardwood whips, fir, red spruce, and brush piles. It became all but impossible to walk anywhere but on roads and cleared trails."

Today's Allagash River experience is probably wilder than in the 19th and early 20th centuries, thank goodness. It's a land that is recovering from the wounds inflected by man, and an experience that people from all over the world appreciate for its natural value—but will that always be the case? Learning from historical records, I gotta believe It is going to take constant vigilance to ensure that the healing process continues.

Reader's Notes:

15
GUM BOOK

Exhausted, Margaret yawned and decided it was time for bed. In case she woke up earlier than normal, the methodical correspondent removed each log book from the box and piled the diaries on the table beside the cardboard box. Margaret arranged the memoirs in chronological order, the newest on the bottom with oldest on top. When she removed the last ranger's journal she saw something in the corrugated container that blended so well with the paper container–it could have been missed.

The same color as the cardboard carton and almost the same size was a wooden book. Not a book in the sense of a hardcover with pages, but a solid block of pine that had been sculpted to resemble a hefty tome. Removing the volume Margaret saw the work was the color of aged leather brown. The four edges of the cover had been etched with rope style webbing. Burned in Algerian lettering about two inches from the top the name **JAMES CLARK** identified the book's owner.

The top, right side, and bottom of the model's edge had been shaped in cavetto style molding to resemble the shape of indented pages. The left edge was rounded to look like a bound work. The woody manuscript would have felt at home on any library book shelf.

Measuring 10 inches by 12 inches, the large curiosity was about 3 inches thick. Margaret removed the discovery and found the handy-work to be substantial. The reporter flipped the book over and saw that the rope design from the front was recreated on the back. Turning the book over Margaret couldn't find any obvious way to open any type of a cover and she wondered *what in the world could this be for? Maybe it was used on a shelf as a book end?*

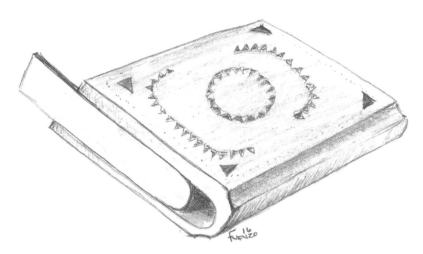

Spruce gum box. Illustration by Frank Manzo, Jr.

After examining the carving, Margaret sat the wooden book on the table. Getting up to place her tea cup in the sink, Margaret's feet slipped on the floor and she fell against the table. The ranger logs scattered across the table surface and the wooden book dangled dangerously close to falling off the edge. Making a grab she clutched the wooden book just before it went over. As she did so, the top edge of the book moved slightly. On closer examination Margaret found that the bottom of the book was solid but the top had a sliding lid to expose a hollowed opening and access to the contents within.

The wooden book, at first thought to be just a library bookshelf decoration, was a type of backwoods safety deposit box, Margaret now realized—and there was something inside. Carefully she removed the contents and found page after page of carefully preserved history.

Forgetting her fatigue, the writer dismissed the lateness of the night as she removed the articles from their safe haven. The investigative reporter was so curious she couldn't call it a night; *nope– not quite yet*. And so she read:

* Author's Note: As early as 1860 Spruce gum boxes were handmade by Maine lumbermen to hold their cherished spruce (chewing) gum. The wooden boxes were typically made from Maine pine and fashioned in the form of small boxes or books; with sliding lids to allow access. The bottom is fixed but the top lid slides open to allow access to the box. As is typical, the front of the box is decorated with a nicely chip carved border.

They are often decorated with chip carvings. Many times these were carved to relieve monotony, loneliness, and tension in crowed lumber camps. Often the boxes would be filled with spruce gum and sent to loved ones back home. Spruce gum boxes are likened to the scrimshaw produced by whalers and represent a distinctly Maine folk art.

Wilderness, Mud, and Two Locomotives
Preservation News from Maine's North Woods
By
Terrence F. Harper
November 1996

From September 14th through September 21st [1996] volunteers from the Allagash Alliance Group raised and stabilized the Eagle Lake & West Branch Railroad No.1 and No. 2., located in the Tramway Historic District in the heart of the Allagash Wilderness Waterway. The project utilized donated equipment and over four hundred hours of volunteer labor and donated equipment in an cooperative effort involving the Allagash Alliance, the Maine Bureau of Parks and Lands, the Allagash Wilderness Waterway, Bureau of General Service, the Maine College Conservation Corp, and the Boy Scouts of America.

The locomotives, situated in a remote location in Maine's northern forest, are part of the remains of the Eagle Lake & West Branch Railroad, a logging railroad built by Great Northern Paper of Millinocket, Maine and a Quebec lumber baron, Edouard "King" LaCroix from St. George, Quebec. Stretching 13 miles from its terminus at the Tramway on Eagle

Lake to Umbazookus Lake with a 5-mile extension to Chesuncook Meadows; the E.L. &W.B operated from 1927 through 1933, hauling pulpwood from the north-flowing Allagash River basin to the southward-flowing currents of the West Branch of the Penobscot River. During its short life span the railroad hauled over 65,000 cords of pulpwood per operating season which ran from spring thaw to fall freeze up.

All equipment for the operation included 30 pulp cars, three 225-foot- long conveyors, included E.L.&W.B. No. 1 a Schenectady built 4-6-0 dating from 1897 and E.L. & W.B. No. 2 was a 2-8-0 built by Brooks in 1902. Both engines were dismantled and moved overland by Lombard Log Haulers. This involved a 50-mile journey over crude logging roads from Lac Frontière, Quebec to the railroad's terminal at Tramway.

In 1933, faced with economic difficulties brought forth by the Depression; the railroad was abandoned. Today the locomotives and the remains of the Tramway are situated in the Tramway Historic District along with the relics of a unique steam-powered conveyor system that operated from 1901–

1908.

The jacking project did not get off to a very auspicious start. The crew stood in the cold rain at John's Bridge and watched boxes full of food disintegrate into mush. The night before, September 13th, they had driven through heavy rain over 80 miles of muddy logging roads. After arriving at the AWW ranger headquarters at Churchill Dam they found out that the person from the Bureau of General Services who was to oversee the removal of the remaining asbestos trapped under the steel shroud of the locomotives had been rushed out to the hospital. Fortunately, his condition was not serious and he returned a few days later. Then, in the morning, two volunteers packed up and headed for home defeated by the weather while the remainder of the crew struggled to move equipment and material to the site. Convincing each other that the project actually began on the 14th rather than Friday the 13th provided no consolation.

Partial Tally of Project Tasks
September 1995–December 1999

· September 1995-removed over 3,000 pounds of asbestos material from the locomotive boilers as well as from a steam Lombard log hauler boiler also located at the site.

· February 1996-moved 100 railroad ties by Allagash Wilderness Rangers and Maine College Conservation Corp.

· September 1996-MCCC excavated jacking pits underneath the locomotives.

Boy Scouts of America with troops from Houlton and Island Falls cleared a trail to a rail pile and improved the trail across the 3,000-foot wide isthmus that separates Eagle and Chamberlain Lakes.

· Transporting of the blocking material by boat which included 500 board feet of 4" x 4" x 3' hardwood blocking; 300 linear feet of 2" x 8" x 10' hardwood planks and 175 linear feet of 1" x 8" x 10' hardwood boards, and hydraulic power units for jacking.

· Transported 150 yards of ballast the hard way. By snowmobile volunteers moved 5,200 five-gallon plastic bucket loads of gravel and stone three miles across the ice of Chamberlain Lake.

- Moving four 100-ton jacks that were powered by a hydraulic pump.
- Over 5,000 hours of volunteer labor

Partial List of Unexpected Challenges

- Mud, rain created jacking pits full of water and mud.
- It was discovered during the jacking that every drive wheel of exhibited spokes that had been broken and crudely welded highlighted the fact that locomotive No. 2-an 2-8-0, weighing 180,000 lbs., was too heavy to be used on the 40 lb. rail that had been built on top of a substandard railroad bed. The locomotive built by Brooks in 1902 had been constructed to pull freight on a well-maintained and ballasted Lake Shore & Michigan Southern, not crude pulp cars through the Maine woods.
- Up jacking it was discovered there was an additional 700 lbs. of asbestos material underneath the trains that had to be removed.
- In Summary

  On June 19th, 1999 with the creak of rusty springs, the dirty red-streaked tender of locomotive

No. 1 settled back to rest on steel rails. In three years volunteers had held cost down from an original estimate cost of $200,000 to an actual expenditure of $20,000. Once the jacking was completed the site was cleaned up and equipment removed by the small fleet to John's Bridge. Soon the whine of chain saws and the drone of the power unit were replaced by the rustle of fall leaves and the hushed whisper of the chilled autumn breeze. In spite of the weather Mother Nature brewed up, the project exceeded expectations. Taking one last look at their accomplishments before heading to the boats, the crew thought, *what better way to enjoy historic railroad preservation than in the middle of the wild splendor of Maine's Allagash Wilderness.*

Leveled Eagle lake and West Branch Locomotive at the Tramway
Photograph courtesy of Bean's Eye View Photography www.
beanseyeview.com

*Author's Note-The information provided in the
excerpt entitled "Wilderness, Mud, and Two Locomotives"
is only a partial discussion of the full reports made to the
Department of Conservation by Terrance F. Harper and David
Hubley, the architects of the herculean effort that stabilized
two historic locomotives in the most remote section of the
Maine woods. The full accomplishments and difficulties that
volunteers overcame under their guidance during a four-
year project may not be fully understood but will always be
appreciated.

Turning the lists of project tasks over Margaret found a another piece of forgotten history, a yellowed account from long ago when one of the locomotives, en route, had tipped off a tote sled, onto its side into the snow—long before it ever hauled even one piece of Maine timber. And there was more…

The NORTHWOODS REPORTER

Patten, Maine,

March 15, 1928

Lombard Log Hauler towing the undercarriage of one of the trains to the Tramway.
From the Terry Harper Collection.

Hello friends, I have just returned from a wonderful trip through the upper St. John and Allagash territory.

After meeting Warden Wood in Fort Kent, we took the 2:00 am Canadian National train to St. Amselme, Quebec, a distance of approximately 200 miles. Nearly all the way at every siding were camps and pulpwood piles which we took as a sign of a prosperous industry. As we traveled north the snow became deeper and deeper. I have never seen so much snow in my life. In some places the snow topped the telegraph poles.

Just south of Quebec City we boarded a Quebec Central train bound for the border town of Lac Frontière where we arrived around 11:00 pm and were glad to be done with it. It seemed that the train stopped at nearly every little crossroad.

After spending the night at a very good hotel we boarded an automobile stage and travelled over the well-plowed roads of Èdouard Lacroix of St. George de Beauce, the lumber king in this part of northern Maine. All along the route we encountered trucks hauling supplies into the camps and the occasional Lombard gasoline tractor laboring to haul trains of tank sleds laden with gasoline and oil as well as sleds loaded with hay for the woods teams and other bulk commodities.

Just after crossing the border we passed a most unusual sight, four huge sleds and a number of Lombard tractors hauling a 188,000-lb. locomotive. A former denizen of the mighty New York Central railroad, it was being moved over 50 miles to Eagle Lake, far from the rails of the famous Broadway Limited, where it will haul pulpwood over the humble rails of Lacroix's 18-mile long Eagle Lake & West Branch railroad which was completed last August. When we again met this strange convoy the next morning they had covered 27 miles to the Clayton Lake Depot camp. We learned later that the locomotive made good progress over the following days with only one delay caused by the sled carrying the boiler sliding off the trail and upsetting. However, this was quickly cleared and the convoy continued on its way.

Facing a 55-mile hike to Ashland, with many stretches that had not seen a track, we moved on toward the Musquacook Lake country. On Glazier Brook we stopped at the camps of Roy & Roy which housed and fed over 200 men during the cutting season. In this district there are 27 lumber camps employing over 2,000 men.

It's a different world here in the realm of "King" Lacroix. In these camps you will hear not a word of English. We did not find any Americans with the exception of three scalers who were placed there by Great Northern Paper Company.

Mr. Lacroix is spoken of very highly wherever we went. Warden Wood informed me that Lacroix has sent word to all his camps that no deer may be used and no guns kept in the camps. It's Warden Wood's observation that this mandate is obeyed pretty well.

This is spruce country and we observed some 200,000 cords of pulpwood and 28 million board feet of long logs being cut this season. We noted that many of the trees are dying or dead from over-maturity and disease and the harvest of this great crop is timely.

Most of the hauling is being done with gasoline Lombard tractors though an occasional steam Lombard log hauler can be found as well. Such is the fervor of this work that the tractors are running night and day with the exception of Sunday which is observed by all.

After leaving Roys' camp we headed for the Great Northern Paper Co. 25-mile depot camp with Supt. T.S. Ranney serving as our host. That bed sure felt good after a tough 22-mile snowshoe trek. Along the way we stopped at the old American Reality depot camp at Mesquacook Lake. Though the buildings have not been in use for the past six years, in the cook-house we found the water still running in the wooden sinks from a great spring in the hill. To think how sweet that water tasted.

The next day I parted ways with Warden Wood. Using the phone line, which fortunately hadn't fallen prey to a moose's antlers, he made arrangements for me to hitch a ride on a Lombard tractor. Huddled in an old horse blanket and sharing the rear platform with drums of gasoline, whose vapors made us light-headed and nauseous we arrived in Ashland in about three hours frozen from the cold and our ears ringing from the staccato bark of the unmuffled exhaust.

The deer were very plentiful around the lumber operations we visited. The fresh cuttings provide them with good food and the roads good footing. The snow in most places measured about 4 feet but is well packed. Partridge however seem scarce and there were few signs of moose.

* These are the conditions I found during my sojourn through a corner of our state far removed from any settlement, where majestic mountains look down upon a snow-covered ocean of spruce.

* Author's Note: Game Warden Wood was the actual author of the above article. He wrote it after touring the warden districts in 1927. Other Fish & Wildlife wardens mentioned in the original article are Chief Warden Roland S. Conners, E.L. Spinney, Henry Taylor (the same as Taylor camps?) and Stanley Gendell.

All the locations are real as well as the names. Unfortunately we don't know which paper it appeared in!

Chère Paulette ,

As-tu reçu l'argent que je t'ai envoyé? S'il te plaît, n'oublie pas de faire le paiement
pour la voiture et de mettre un petit quelque chose de côté et peut-être quelques
bonbons à la cenne pour les enfants. Si tu viens nous visiter , tu devras acheter un billet
au bureau de la compagnie à St-Georges. Tu peux embarquer dans un camion de
livraison en partant du Lac Frontière jusqu'au Churchill. Habilles-toi chaudement et
apporte une oreiller pour t'asseoir parce que les chemins sont rudes et ces chauffeurs
vont vite!

Après les évènements qui se sont produits l'autre nuit, j'ai cru que nous serions pris
pour vivre sur notre petit compte d'épargne. Tu vois, moi et mon "striker" (la personne
qui se déplace avec moi pour accrocher et décrocher les traineaux) nous descendions le
Long Lake vers les camps Roy. Au moment ou nous sommes arrivés à Grey Brook pour
graisser et huiler le tracteur, j'étais gelé et mort de fatigue. Je ne suis pas encore
habitué au quart de nuit. Avec une courte saison de halage, nous devons faire
fonctionner le tracteur vingt- quatre heures par jour, six jours par semaine pour que les
billots soient arrivés à destination avant que les routes de glace ne dégèlent. Aussi,
j'étais étourdi par le bruit d'échappement. Nous nous emplissons les oreilles avec des
boules de coton mais en travaillant à plein régime, tu peux entendre un de ces tracteurs
Lombard à une distance de trois miles, cela me rappelle le son de nos mitrailleuses
Lewis lorsque nous étions dans les tranchées en France , c'était assourdissant.

Alors que je travaillais autour du tracteur, je me suis souvenu que Joe m'avais dit que le
cuisinier du camp Blanchette à Grey Brook faisait les meilleures tartes. Dans l'état ou
nous étions, notre décision est venue rapidement. Après avoir fermer la valve du
radiateur, nous avons laissé le tracteur tourner au ralenti sur la glace. En remontant le
ruisseau, nous sommes vite arrivés au camp et comme promis, le cuistot nous
attendait avec un festin de tartes fraîchement cuisinées , des beignes et une tasse de
café pendant que l'on se réchauffait près du poêle.

En retournant vers le lac, nous étions surpris de ne pas voir les lumières du tracteur. La première chose que l'on a pensé, c'est qu'il s'était arrêté tout seul. À -20 degré comme cette nuit-là, redémarrer le moteur aurait été un vrai cauchemar. Tu vois, lorsque le moteur est refroidi et que l'huile s'est épaissie , le démarreur électrique ne peut le faire tourner. Alors, il faut le faire tourner à la main et quelquefois, il faut se mettre à deux pour réussir.

Puis, nous avons réalisé que remettre le tracteur en marche était le moindre de nos soucis. À l'endroit où devait se trouver le Lombard , il n'y avait rien d'autre qu'un grand trou dans la glace! M. Lessard a demandé à notre chef mécanicien, Emile Labbé, de construire une grosse structure en tronc d'arbres au dessus du trou et M. Ferland le forgeron a façonné quatre gros crochets. Ils ont fait venir un plongeur de la côte. Le tracteur était descendu 40 pieds sous l'eau et il a fallu plusieurs essais avant de réussir à le remonter. Pendant tout ce temps, nous avons dû nous relayer pour tourner la manivelle du compresseur. Heureusement, M. Lessard a dit à M. Lacroix qu'il y avait une source sous la glace à l'endroit où le tracteur était arrêté et c'est pourquoi la glace était mince. Il ne lui a rien dit au sujet des beignes et des tartes! Quel gentil homme que ce M. Lessard.

Ton Edgar

Bonjour Mon Chère Paulett,

I write this to you this in francais, but I aaussi wish to try in anglais. The American language is new to moi, but I espèrer to do ok. Ok?

Did you receive the money I sent to vous? Don't forget to make the payment on the automobile and put a petit something in savings and perhaps some Am cent bonbons for the kids? S'il te plait.

If you come up to visit you will need to buy a ticket at the Company office in St. George. You can ride in one of the supply trucks from Lac Frontière to Churchill. Bundle up warm and bring a pillow to sit on–the road is rough and those drivers go fast!

I thought we would be living off our little saving account after the events of a few la nuits ago. You see my Striker and moi (the man who rides on top with me to hitch and unhitch the sleds) were driving down Long Lake to Les Camps Roy. By the time we arriver to Grey Brook and stopped to grease and oil the tractor I was frozen and dead with de fatigue. I am still not use to the nuit shift. With only a bref hauling season we have to run the tractor twenty four heure per day, six days per week to get logs landed before ice roads break-up. I was also numb from the exhaust noise. We stuff le cottan in our ears but working at full throttle you can hear one of these Lombard tractors nearly 3 miles away. It reminds me of being in the trenches in France and the sound of our section's

Lewis machine gun–only for hours on end.

As I worked around the tractor I remembered Joe telling me that the cook at Blanchett's Grey Brook camp made the best tartes. Being in the condition we have, it didn't take us long to decide. After closing the radiator shutter we left the tractor idling out on the ice. Hiking up the brook we were soon at the camp and as promised the cookie had us feasting on fresh baked pie, donut and a cup of coffee while we warm-up by the stove.

Hiking back to the lac we were surprised that we couldn't see the headlights from the tractor. Our first thought was that it had stalled. I can't even begin to tell you how dreadful that is. Especially when it's 20 degrees lower than zero as it was that night. You see once the engine cools off the oil gets thick like molasses, and the electric starter can't make it go. Then we have to crank it by hand – sometimes it takes two of us, quoi!

Than we realized getting the tractor started again was the least of our worries–sa cré bleu. Where the Lombard should have been there was nothing but a big hole in the ice! Mr. Lessard had our master mechanic, Emile Labbé build a gross timber frame built over the hole and four big hooks made by the blacksmith Mr. Fernald. They hired a diver to come up from the coast. The tractor, as we say se baignent-go for a dip in 40 feet deep of water, oh merde! It took several tries to get it out.

All the time, even da game warden and the rest of us had to take turns cranking the diver's l'air compressor. Thankfully Mr. Lessard told Mr. Lacroix that where the tractor had stopped there was a spring that had caused thin ice. He didn't tell him about the donuts and the pie! What a bon man Mr. Lessard is! Tout fini.

        Ton Edgar

Lombard under ice.
Photograph from the Terry Harper Collection.

Author's Note: Except for Paulett all of the people mentioned above were part of the 1927 LaCroix work force. Augustus Lessard was LaCroix's superintendent, Emile Labbe was a master mechanic, Mr. Fernal was the blacksmith at the Tramway during the summer and at Churchill Village during the winter, Edgar was a tractor driver. Lombard log haulers, first built in 1901, had a top speed of 5 miles per hour, could haul 125 cord of wood, were steamed powered and weighed an average of 15-ton. Due to the maneuverability of the log hauler the six-year operation of the tramway came to an end.

Lombard Log hauler being hauled to surface after going through the ice near Gray Brook on Long Lake T11R13.   Photograph from the

Terry Harper Collection.

Steel helmet diver Photograph from the Terry Harper Collection.

Horse and sleigh in front of derrick. Photograph from the Terry Harper Collection.

Reader's Notes:

16
SIX DEGREES

The next morning, the day being Friday and the start of the weekend, Margaret arrived at Pleasant Ridge at her usual time and grabbed coffee from the carafe in the dayroom and, at the urging of the nurse, walked through the open door of Jim's room.

Jim had been sitting in the oak captain's chair and turned to greet her with a smile and said, "Nice to see ya. Glad you found the coffee. Have a seat." Without waiting for a response, he continued "You ever heard of six degrees of separation, Maggie?" Jim watched Margaret's body language for any sign of nervousness.

"Don't think so," she replied, wondering where the elderly man was going this time, so early in the interview, too. In the preceding hours of questions and answers, Margaret had found Jim to be of sound mind. Despite his physical age, his thoughts came sharp and clear and he was quick to grasp onto any subject like the proverbial steel trap.

"It's a theory really, but it sure seems to be accurate." Rising to offer more of the hot brew from his metal coffee pot percolator, Margaret waved off her refill so Jim filled his cup and returned the vessel to the hot plate, and continued. "Basically the hypothesis is that everyone and everything is only six steps or fewer away from each other."

Seeing the puzzled look on Margaret's face, Jim explained, "For example, you are introduced to someone and learn they are someone who knows your family or one of your friends. Try it next time you're out in a crowd. Talk with a complete stranger and more often than not you'll find a common connection."

"So do I just go up to any stranger and ask, 'Who do you know that I might know?'"

Sensing skepticism Jim smiled and said, "Nah, just start talking with anyone about any generic subject. For example, ask people where they are from, or about their hobbies. Often such inquiries will lead to the connection to someone you both know."

"And I want to know this because…?" said Margaret as she stopped scribing and wondered where he was going with all of this and why now.

"Do you remember when I told you about the penny amulet that I found near the Ice Caves?" Margaret nodded to indicate that she remembered.

So Jim continued, "And how I went into the caves and the scenes that flickered on the cavern wall from the past and that I was able to see into the future?"

Agreeing, Margaret replied, "Yes I do. But frankly it all sounded like a tall tale. A good one, but nevertheless; a yarn."

"I can see why you'd think that, but it was all true." Jim emphasized. "And there is more."

Moving his chair closer to Margaret so he could bend at the waist to grasp her hand, Jim, in a mystical voice asked, "Was your mother's first husband named George?"

Nervously, Margaret replied, "Yes it was but how…?"

Jim then looked deep into her eyes and inquired, "Is your middle name Sanborn?"

Margaret was stunned. Letting go of Jim's hand and sitting straight back in her chair dumbfounded.

The woman had never told anyone her middle name. Heck, she didn't even know where it had come from, her mom had never said. *How, how could Jim possibly know?*

"Margaret, listen closely, please! My great-grandfather was a Sanborn. His first name was Joseph and he was the seventh son of a seventh son. It was he who blessed our family with the pentacle—our good luck charm—and left it at the ice caves on Allagash Lake."

Just when Margaret thought the conversation couldn't get any weirder, Jim squeezed her hand a little harder to emphasis the words to come next.

"You need to recover the coin. In my visit to the Ice Cave, so long ago, I saw you were coming. At the time I didn't know who you were, when, or why you would arrive, but I saw you and I saw why you need the luck the penny can bring."

"What is going to happen to me?" Margaret asked, now feeling very nervous.

"Let's just say, it's not about what happens as much as what doesn't happen if you don't retrieve the coin, that matters."

"I am confused. It's what's not going to happen that's important? But …"

And before she could finish, the nurse entered the room and interrupted, "I am sorry to bother, but the doctor is here and he needs to speak with Mr. Clark about the results from his recent tests."

Rising, Jim said, "Ok I am coming." And then he turned to Margaret and said emphatically, "The stone. Go to my Grampy's Jim's grave."

Margaret, stunned by the recent revelation, hollered after Jim as he left to ask, "Where, where is the stone?"

From down the hall Margaret heard Jim answer, "It's marked on the map. Look at the map on the desk. Take the chart with you."

Reader's Notes:

17
ROAD NUMBER SIX, ROW 9, PLOT 16

With Jim's revelation heavy on her mind
Margaret picked up the map and walked down the hall
toward the entrance. Outside, through the glass entry,
Margaret saw that the sunny day had soured into a
stormy gray. Skies were overcast and a cold rain had
begun. Putting the atlas inside her day pack to protect
the diagram from the drizzle, Margaret ran to her car,
dodging rain drops as best she could. Relieved when
the car roared to life with the first turn of the key,
thank goodness, she thought and put the car into gear
and headed onto the highway.

Turning left rather than right and back to
the rent, Margaret drove toward I95 where she
would travel until reaching Route 2 in the hamlet of
Newport. Once on Route 2, the Canaan Road, she

continued west driving parallel with the Kennebec River and the famous Arnold Trail to her south. Passing by the watercourse Margaret thought she could hear the tremolo call of the common loon predicting a severe storm. Once she crossed the Skowhegan town line and passed by Eaton Mountain, Margaret turned right on the East Ridge Road and toward the little settlement of Cornville.

Continuing north she reached the four corners of the Huff Road and the Ames Road, only a hop, skip and jump from the historic Cornville Grange, and the village cemetery. She pulled up to the only entrance to the consecrated ground. To the right of the graveyard, Margaret noticed a white, single-story building that once had been a church, and a very busy place.

Constructed in 1825, the front of the wooden cathedral had two front doors facing the road. One entry opened on the left side of the building and the other on the right. The entrances served as a reminder of a time when proper Puritan etiquette required men to enter through one door and women the other; so they would be separated during the sermon. The decision had been made because, according to religious doctrine of the time, "there weren't any marriages in heaven."

Margaret parked beside a green truck that had an official appearing decal on the door that identified the pickup as a vehicle of the State Department of Inland Fisheries and Wildlife.

Slipping on a raincoat to protect against the increasing storm, Margaret followed the directions on the map into the burial ground. At one time the final resting place had boasted of a steel wrought iron gate and fence but now that railing had been replaced by a white fence, more in keeping with the history of the once important dairy farms, now that cattle didn't roam at will.

Choosing the center road that bisected the old churchyard, Margaret walked down the sandy drive until she found road number 6, row 9 and walked toward plot 16; in search of a grave. In a short time she found the inscription she'd been told about:

JAMES PAUL CLARK

BORN NOVEMBER 16, 1938

DIED JUNE 1, 1993

THE SPIRIT STILL LINGERS IN A

FOREST PLACE...

Looking over the sea of stone, Margaret saw a solitary figure standing silent, head bowed near the monument. Walking softly so as not to interrupt the only other person in the consecrated ground during a time of reflection, Margaret was puzzled to see the man standing in front of the same memorial stone that she'd been told to locate. The stranger had knelt with his right forearm resting on one knee. Quietly she approached the grass plot only to see the visitor stand and turn. Margaret saw he was wearing a type of uniform and recognized the bronze badge pinned over his left shirt pocket identified him as a Maine Game Warden. Wearing a long sleeve shirt, the coatless man seemed oblivious to the inclement weather.

The warden was so deep in thought that he acted surprised to see the pretty lady standing so close. Appraising the newcomer for any sign of hostility, his trained eye immediately realized that she didn't pose a threat. He nodded and smiled, and walked back toward the parking lot.

As the man passed, Margaret read the name tag pinned over the seam of the right pocket of the uniform, and saw the man's name was Dennis James. Recognizing man's last name, she wondered, *could he be related to Jim's old friend Dalton James,* but quickly let the thought go. Moving easily, the man left without a word. A southerly gust carried the blended aroma of softwood smoke and Ole Woodsman's Fly Dope from the woodsman to the reporter.

Margaret drew closer to the stone of Jim's grandfather that she has heard so much about and searched for any hint of a sign that would determine her fate. Now alone in the burial ground, with distant thunder rumbling, Margaret shivered at the change in the weather.

To the south, an angry black cloud approached, the wind picked up speed, and a spinning dirt devil loosened an exterior shutter from the side of the old church. Once freed, the closure exposed the glass of a window of the old church. Banging loudly against the side of historic building; the slapping of wood against wood was the only noise heard above the intensifying thunderstorm.

Running her hand across the face of the stone, the lettering felt cold and distant to her touch. She looked for a mark of a coin or ribbon or any other talisman to indicate her luck, an omen she'd been told to locate. After 20 minutes, with a full-blown gale building and no signal in sight, Margaret headed back to the safety of her car.

When Margaret approached the car from the passenger side, the only living sole in the cemetery on a dark night, noticed that the right front tire on her car had gone flat. *Great!* Margaret thought. *I've never changed a tire in my life. Guess I'd better call road-side assistance.* Sliding behind the steering wheel, Margaret pulled out her cellphone to dial the 1-800-number but there wasn't any signal. Examining her phone under the illumination of the car's interior lighting, Margaret saw that her lifeline had a dead battery.

The black sky opened and heavy rain pounded the ground. Sitting behind the steering wheel she stared through the windshield at the moisture pelting from the heavens. Gale force winds rocked the car from side to side.

Now what do I do, spend the night in the car and hope someone comes by? I'm not walking anywhere in this storm. Margaret's thought was interrupted by a lightning bolt that struck the ground inside the middle of the cemetery. Within an instant a bright light appeared in the now visible window of the church, like a glow from a neon sign, lettering flashed across the window, identified the area as *The Old Burial Ground* and disappeared.

Curious to see if there would be someone, or somebody inside that would let her use a phone, Margaret pulled the hood of the raincoat over her head and exited the car. Drawing closer to the sanctuary, the light inside faded and went out. *Either my imagination or reflection from the lightning,* Margaret rationalized, *Guess, I prefer to think it was a reflection.* Returning to the only shelter she had, the car. Margaret traced her steps back through the soaked grass when to her right she saw a red glow emanating from inside the fenced enclosure, specifically from road number 6, row 9, plot 16.

Reader's Notes:

18
FROM 1838

Walking toward the radiant light, the storm softly quieted and the rain calmed to a gentle mist. The evening's temperature warmed just enough so a person exposed to the outside elements wouldn't be cold. But Margaret didn't notice.

Shimmering red, the stone could have been mistaken for the soothing warmth of a welcoming campfire, if it hadn't been in the middle of a graveyard, in the middle of the night, in the middle of a thunderstorm. Moving slowly, as if summoned by telepathy Margaret felt pulled by an invisible force.

When she drew close to the headstone, a reflective illumination appeared on the face of the marker. Falling to her knees for a better look, she removed her coat's hood and didn't even notice that the grass wasn't wet, nor did she observe that the rain was falling around her, but not on her. She didn't notice that the name of James Paul Clark, now displayed boldly across the face of the granite memorial. She didn't even notice the vehicle that had pulled into the parking lot and stopped beside her car.

What she did detect was the scene that displayed across the face of the stone. Similar to the coming attractions preview one might see at a movie theater, Margaret recognized her own features, while scenarios of her life, past and future flashed in fast forward time across the flat surface of the gray stone. After only minutes, the movie flickered and faded. Within seconds the stone had reverted to its normal gray, when Margaret heard a voice call, "Madam, **madam, hey lady**, are you ok?"

"Huh? Yeah I'm fine." *I guess* she thought, keeping that notion to herself.

Then she saw the talisman appear. As the footsteps from behind drew closer, Margaret reached out to remove a 1838 copper penny, attached to a blue ribbon from its position, dangling from the stone of James P. Clark.

Slipping the coin pendant into her coat pocket, she turned and saw the uniform of Warden Dennis

James; the man who'd been at the gravesite when she arrived. Coming to her senses that she wasn't alone any longer, Margaret asked, "Why? But how did…? Why did you come back?"

"Don't really know for sure. I just got this funny feeling, like I had left something behind. I only got about 10 miles down the road, when I felt the need to return. Glad I did. When I saw your car with a flat tire, and the grounds completely dark; I got worried that something may have happened."

"Did you see the radiance by this stone?"

"Lady, except for lightening and the headlights of my truck, I haven't seen any lights since the storm hit. Did you fall? You look like you're in shock. Slipping and hitting your head can cause confusion."

Relieved to find an excuse Margaret quickly confirmed, "Yes that's probably it. I must have slipped on the wet grass."

The rain continued to intensify so the warden suggested, "Let's go back to my truck and get out of the weather." Grabbed by a firm hand, Margaret allowed herself to be pulled along back to the vehicles, to a place of shelter, never once remembering to pull the hood of the raincoat back over her head.

The torrent intensified and by the time they had reached the parking lot, Margaret had been bombarded so by the rain-turned-sleet that her hair was coated with pellets of ice so heavy that the hail had carpeted the ground.

"We're soaking wet, what do you say we grab a coffee? I don't know about you, but I haven't eaten since lunch and sure could use a burger. I'll help you change the tire when the storm lets up."

"That sounds good actually," Margaret said with her recent experience replaying through her mind. *Just to sit still for a minute would feel really nice right now and not to be alone. I really don't want to be alone!*

*****

Pulling into the parking lot of the first restaurant they found in Skowhegan, the two took a seat at a table in the popular Heritage House eatery.

They immediately ordered a carafe of coffee, and over burgers and salad Margaret explained to her new friend about where she was from, what she did for work, and only that she had visited the graveyard as a follow-up to her writing assignment on Jim Clark.

Margaret learned that Dennis had been a game warden with the Maine Fish and Wildlife Service for 10 years. Warden James was assigned to the Chamberlain Lake District and "Yes he was very familiar with Allagash Lake, and often patrolled there."

Dennis explained that he was single and the grandson of Dalton James, the Allagash ranger who had been a close friend with a Mr. Jim Clark, the man now buried in the Cornville cemetery. It had been Dalton James, who had first shown the current Mr. Jim Clark of the Pleasant Ridge Assisted Living Community the ropes.

Grandfather Dalton had taught his grandson Dennis all there was to know about the Maine woods and encouraged the young protégé to become a conservation officer. Dennis was on the way back through Skowhegan after teaching a week-long evidence course at the Maine Criminal Justice Academy to a batch of raw recruits. Margaret also learned that Dennis's grandfather had asked him to visit Mr. Clark's grave whenever he passed by so that their friendship would not be forgotten between the two families.

By midnight, they had returned to Margaret's car, plugged and pumped air into the previously flat tire so the car was now prepared for the trip back to Bangor. Margaret shook his hand, thanked the handsome, black-haired young warden for his help and said good-by with, "It was a pleasure to meet you."

Dennis smiled, "Pleasure's all mine to be sure. By the way I get to Bangor every once in a while, would you want to go out for dinner and a movie sometime?"

Blushing, Margaret was glad the darkness hid the red that now flushed into her cheeks; as one of the images she had seen on the Clark stone replayed through her mind. Nodding without speaking; Margaret reached into the pocket of her coat and gave Dennis a Penobscot Basin Times business card; the only thing she carried that revealed her personal telephone number. Climbing into the car, her cell phone blinked to life.

At 2 A.M. Margaret walked through the door of her one-room apartment and she thought the low income rent looked perfect on this fine Saturday morning. Hanging her wet things over the back of a kitchen chair, she emptied the pockets of her raincoat, and placed the ipad in its work location at the table, near the coffeemaker.

Margaret wasn't scheduled to be back at

Pleasant Ridge until 7 A.M. Monday morning so she planned to sleep in.

Reader's Notes:

19
WHAT A WAY TO SPEND A DAY OFF

Rising at noon Margaret felt refreshed. She had the rest of Saturday and all day Sunday to herself. *But what to do?* she wondered as a range of options threaded through her mind. Absentmindedly Margaret thought about going to the mall to look for a sale on walking shoes, or maybe she could take in a movie *I think I have enough money for a matinée,* the girl reasoned. Pouring a cup of coffee she briefly thought about yesterday's encounter with Dennis and considered, *sure would be nice to have a friend to go with.*

While Margaret considered plans for the day, she opened her ipad to check her Facebook page for any news from her old college roommate. Finding nothing, Margaret closed the protective cover, and saw the box of Jim's diaries patiently calling out from their shelf space along the far side of the table.

From the diary of James Clark

Suzie the Muskrat

Early this morning I'd left the Churchill Dam's ranger camp and begun the day's patrol across Churchill Lake, when I stumbled onto a most unusual situation.

The day had started like any other for someone living in a cabin in the Maine wilderness. My living room window overlooked a small blue pond that formed the headwater of the turbulent Chase Rapids. The calendar said that we were nearing the end of March and spring was in the air. Ducks had returned to the only open water available. The migratory fowl were quacking in pleasure as they swam and dove in the shadow of Churchill Dam.

March is my second favorite month in the woods [October being the first]; a time when Mother Nature casts off the blanketing shroud of old man winter.

Cold nights turn into the fresh air of bright sunny days. Early in the morning the snow base is frozen hard enough that travel by either snowshoes or snowmobiling is most pleasant. Cloudless skies are effervescent blue, softwoods are a vibrant green; a picturesque setting made vivid by the mounds of white snow.

Animals are escaping from their winter sleep; red squirrels chase and scold one another throughout the red bark tops of the hemlock trees. White-tails are searching melted plots of ground in search of new green grass to replace their winter diet of the aromatic white cedar. Raccoons, skunks, and black bears increase their level of activity and show their presence. The hide of the majestic moose has molted and remains quite patchy until the coarse hair becomes a lighter, summer coat. It is a time of new life, a time of rebirth.

I had begun the day's snowmobile patrol to ensure that folks were ok, ice shacks had been removed before the spring thaw, and retrieve any litter that had been left behind.

When I entered the wide part of Churchill lake I spied two snowmobiles of a party fishing about 200 feet off the mouth of Churchill Brook. A warming fire had been built near shore and wispy smoke from the flames climbed straight into the cloudless sky,

As I approached, I noticed that a person was rolling around on the ice, moving their arms and legs-using a long stick to slap at the lake's surface. A man, appearing unconcerned, was jigging through the ice for lake trout and watching flailing of a person who turned out to be the man's wife. A young girl in a pink snowmobile suit sat on a snowmobile keeping one eye on the person rolling around while she kept the other on the lowered flag of a wooden fishing trap.

I pulled up to the man holding the jig stick, killed the engine of my snowsled, pointed at the woman on the ice and asked, "What's happenin'?"

About that time the lady. Laughing, had returned to her family in time to hear my question. Lightly the wife answered my inquiry.

"Early this morning my husband, daughter, and I left our camp on Spider Lake for a day of fishing. We had just gotten holes drilled and traps set, when this muskrat came out of the tree line by the mouth of the brook, and walked straight toward us. When the rodent got close enough to see what we were, the furbearer hunkered down in the snow and just stared at us. After about an hour, I got concerned that the furbearer might be sick, so I grabbed a long stick for protection and walked over to take a closer look.

"Well the little musky smelling creature didn't care much for having someone so close, so it began a high-pitched squeak and then jumped on my snowsuit; trying to bite me. I got to laughing; my feet got tangled in the snow and I tripped and fell. Once down, the muskrat jumped on my leg, while I swung the stick to keep the grumpy animal at bay. Fortunately, my suit was thick enough so that even the razor sharp three-quarter of an inch long rodent's teeth couldn't penetrate the fabric. After a while the animal stopped its attack."

After enjoying the exploit, I wished the family luck with their fishing and continued my patrol, while the muskrat remained unmoving, trying to use its poor eyesight to focus on these intruders to its world.

Four hours later, I passed by that same spot and saw the family had left, and in the distance the sun shone off the silvery-brown fur of the little 3 pound rodent that had continued on its way across the wide part of Churchill, in a direct line toward Pleasant Stream.

I am not sure where she was headed, but later that summer Suzie, as the critter became known, was often seen swimming across the lake to the opposite shore. Guess everything needs a vacation from time to time.

Suzie the Muskrat on attack. Illustration by Frank Manzo. Jr.

Closing the diary, Margaret picked up the next book, opened to the first entry and read:

From the diary of James Clark

Colder Than Cold

The thermometer fastened to the outside east wall of the camp warned it was bitter cold outside. The liquid mercury had retreated so far down inside the glass stem that a person just knew that beyond the walls of the log cabin, there was a bone chilling, teeth rattling, subzero, unfriendly world. At minus 25 degrees the glacial air of February was made even harsher by a relentless 20 MPH northwest wind. It was so cold that all outdoorsmen were held hostage by the arctic blasts. Snowmobilers and fishermen alike were not moving beyond the circle of radiant heat of their glowing woodstoves.

I had spent days in the camp office doing endless administrative paperwork, and huddling as close to the firebox as possible. One night about nine o'clock, my wife and I looked out the window to see that the light of a brilliant moon had turned the frozen night into day. The wind had died some, so we decided to take a short walk out onto Umsaskis Lake.

That morning I had cut through the ice on the lake and found that surface ice had frozen to a thickness of about three feet, so we weren't concerned about breaking through. Bundled in our warmest wool clothing we waded through the deep snow, down the bank and out onto the glacial tundra. Reaching the ice, we found that the snow on the lake had been packed by the wind and was so crisp, our footsteps sounded like we were walking on layers of frozen eggshells; our breath immediately vaporized and disappeared in the dry air.

About 200 feet offshore, we were over the fishing hole known as togue alley, when the northern lights began pulsating with such brilliance on the horizon, we thought we were seeing the illumination of Quebec City. As we stood, looking up, mesmerized by nature's fireworks, we were suddenly shaken by a massive expanse of ice that cracked directly under our feet.

The sound came so loud and so fast that the resounding rumble roared like a cannon. The sonic boom began behind us, from the south and built towards the north with such force that a two-inch wide gap of a birthing pressure ridge cracked open between our legs. Thinking that the lake, hungry from days of making ice, was opening frosty jaws to swallow us whole, we nearly jumped out of our boots. We listened as the noise thundered and grumbled down Umsaskis in a dash to reach Long Lake Dam, seven miles to the north.

Relieved that we were safe and yet exhilarated by another north woods experience, my wife and I turned and followed our tracks now well-lit by the yellow beacon of the light reflected through the cabin's picture window.

Margaret then picked up the next book in succession and read about unusual weather forecast:

From the diary of James Clark

The Seagull Prediction

Dear log,

From all appearances, spring is on the way. The area is experiencing warm days and cold nights. A light breeze blows across the needles of the spruce, forcing the evergreens to sway under a brilliant sun.

Freed from the bondage of their winter homes, deer are out and about as they feed on sunny patches of grass along the edge of the Telos Road. Partridge are eating new buds from the yellow birch and ducks have claimed ownership of any water free of ice. The fresh smell of springtime tickles the nose.

This is the first week of April and today I took my last snowmobile ride of the year. I can't believe that the winter has passed so quickly.

Two weeks ago the boss transferred me back to Chamberlain ranger's station where I am to prepare for spring fishermen. I expect to be here until it's time to return to Allagash Lake.

Yesterday I took one final patrol of the lakes to ensure that all of the winter's ice shacks had been removed. During the patrol I also inventoried campsites for winter damage, and made a list of spring on tent sites. The lakes are still locked in by ice; but with the warming daylight temperatures, it won't take much of a northwest wind and rain to begin the ritual of spring breakup.

On my way up the lake, I stopped into Nugent's Sporting Camps. The co-owner, Stella, offered her usual "Do you have time for coffee?" And without waiting for an answer she led the way across the yard toward the main lodge.

Partway across the lawn Stella pointed at a rock out cropping in the lake about three-quarters of a mile to the north. A gray ledge void of snow stood out against the icy white surface. Following her lead I looked at the rock and heard Stella say' "The gulls returned today. I figure that ice-out will occur about May 5th."

Early in my career I'd learned that for many years woodsmen have observed weather patterns and habits of wildlife to predict the coming weather. But this was the first time I had heard of such a method of estimating ice-out. So once seated at the historic split log kitchen table I asked her to explain. Stella talked as she poured hot coffee into thick ceramic cups. The brew was complemented by a platter of fresh from the frying pan buttermilk doughnuts.

The lady of the lake explained that Al and Patty Nugent first began building Nugent's Sporting Camps in 1936.

During open water of that year

"Nuge" as Al was called, constructed and launched a 40' by 50' raft from the old Telos Landing. Once in the water the float was loaded with all of Nugent's worldly belongings, which included a piano and a Star Kineo wood cookstove. The couple floated the barge north on Telos Lake and finally reached the outlet of 18-mile long Chamberlain Lake. Four miles farther, the couple came ashore just south of Little Leadbetter Brook. There the couple began the task of creating a home in the wilderness.

It was probably in the spring of 1937 that they first noticed the unusual occurrence that some call today the seagull prediction.

Records from the National Oceanographic Atmospheric Administration (NOAA) weather office in Caribou indicate that the first fifteen days of May 1937 were quite warm. Those two weeks had a high temp of 74 degrees, a low of 23 degrees with an average temperature of 54 degrees. More than likely it was during the last two weeks of April that Nuge and Patty heard a commotion coming from the ledge island. And, as woodsmen and women are apt to do, they probably made a note in their diary.

It was probably early one warm spring morning when Al was standing on the shore by the stream thinking about where he should build a boat dock, when he first heard a commotion booming down the ice-covered surface. Hollering to Patty to "come look and bring the field glasses," Nuge stared north at the white mass of ice. Above the horizon Allagash Mountain stood out as a backdrop against a sparkling dark blue sky.

Within minutes Patty was at his side and Nuge reached for the field glasses she offered. Focusing on the gray ledge the husband and wife took turns watching the seagulls fly around and land on the exposed island in the snow. The coastal birds built nests, scavenged, and argued over such delicacies as fish innards and remnants of winter-killed wildlife.

It was probably that night after supper that Patty noted the seagulls in her daily diary, a log she kept for the remainder of her life.

Most likely it was two or three years later, in rereading her diary notations, that Patty noticed that coincidently, the ice left the lake about 30 days after the seagulls landed on the ledge.

Every year since, the residents of the lake have watched for the return of the gulls and each spring 30 days from when the birds land on the gray outcroppin'; the lake will be free of ice.

And that is the story of how the local landmark on Chamberlain Lake became known as Gull Rock, a name the outcropping still carries today.

"Spring Breakup"

photograph courtesy of Rob and Stella Flewelling. April 2015
Nugent's Chamberlain Lake Camps T7R12

www.nugentscamps.com

Reader's Notes:

20
DOWN THE UPPER STREAM

It's late April and Jim had completed the last patrol of the winter; and the time had come for him to return to the Allagash Lake District, but he can't; the most remote lake in the Allagash Wilderness Waterway was still locked in by ice. So Jim spent the days at the Chamberlain Lake ranger's station waiting for open water. He prepared boats, outboard motors and chainsaws for work that came with the spring thaw because with warmer temperatures came fisherman and with fisherman came *well you just never knew!* Jim had discovered. And warmer weather was on the way.

At Chamberlain Bridge, the thoroughfare was completely free of ice as far north as the Arm and to the south there was open water about a mile into Round Pond. Three weeks before, the seagulls had returned to Gull Rock and so, if the legend was accurate, ice-out was imminent. Jim had just about finished with the spring start up when he received a radio call from the Department of Conservation's Greenville radio dispatch.

The radio operator advised that Currier's Flying Service on Moosehead Lake was on the phone and they had information about ice conditions. That morning pilot Roger Currier had flown over the chain of lakes and he'd found that "Upper Allagash Stream was wide open and flowing heavily. And the upper end of Allagash Lake," the dispatcher had shared, "is free of ice from the inlet east beyond Sandy Point campsite. The rest of the lake is still icebound except for open water by the outlet and around the Five Islands. "

Jim inquired, "Did Roger see anyone on the Ledge Point and Sandy Point campsites, near the Inlet?"

"10-4. Both campgrounds had people. From the air he counted 8 canoes."

"Thank you for the information," replied the ranger. As Jim thought about people on the lake, the ranger automatically considered his options, but he knew there was only one.

Jim remembered that the Ledges could accommodate three groups and Sandy could handle two parties so that meant that the campsites were probably over full. The time had come to return to his summer camp.

"Are you going in?" the dispatcher inquired.

"10-4," replied Jim, "please notify Currier's I'll be on the lake within two days." *Each year too many people capsized in the cold water for a ranger not to be there,* Jim silently rationalized.

"The flying service also advises that while most of the ice in the lake is dark, there is still white ice along the shore in front of your camp." From experience Jim knew that dark colored ice meant the flow had rotted and with a good wind, could go any time. But the white ice, that was a different story. White coloration meant solid ice. Within two days Jim had loaded all of his supplies, two-way radio, his personal canoe, a 17-foot Atkinson Traveler, into the 4x4 truck. At dawn he headed toward his summer assignment and the 20-foot patrol canoe stored at camp.

After several hours of banging over muddy logging roads ripe with frost heaves, blowdowns and washed out culverts, the ranger arrived at the put-in at upper Allagash Stream. There were five other vehicles already there.

Jim walked the 100 feet to the stream and noticed the flow was at a stage typical to an early spring runoff, a torrent that reached from bank to bank. *Looks to be a quick trip today,* he reasoned. *I'll have to watch for sweepers, wouldn't due to go over, and I don't need a dunking. Bet that flow is cold. Water can't be warmer than 36 degrees.*

Making one last radio call before going 10-7 [out of service] Jim called his boss.

"1703 to 1700."

"10-3, 1703." Ranger Supervisor Leigh Smith immediately answered. He'd monitored the conversation with the flying service and understood where Jim was headed.

"I'm ready to head down the stream and into the lake. I am shutting my radio off and will be out of communication. Currier's reports there is still ice in front of camp so I may have to try and walk across it,"

Jim advised and continued. "If you don't hear from me in about three hours, you might want to send in an aircraft to check on me."

"10-4, Jim, I understand. If I haven't received a call from you in three hours, I will fly in with the aircraft."

"10-4, thanks Leigh. 1703 is 10-7." And with that Jim checked the time on his watch and turned off his only connection to the outside world. Back at the park office Leigh understood the danger Jim faced and so he did the only thing a supervisor could do at the moment. He made a phone call and put an aircraft on alert and then he paced the floor and waited.

*****

After Jim removed the canoe from the truck's canoe racks and loaded it at the put-in with enough weight in the bow to balance the craft. He then donned his state-issued green, full-length, long-sleeved coast guard-approved lifejacket thankful that his boss had provided this extra piece of survival protection for all of the rangers. Then he made sure that his two-way radio was secure in a waterproof floatable bag. *I can't afford to have my life-line ruined*, he reasoned.

Jim then placed his left foot in the center of the waiting craft, bent at the waist and placed his hands on both gunwales, and brought in his right foot over the starboard side. Once balanced, the woodsman kneeled on the floor in front of the stern seat of the Traveler, grabbed his paddle, and swung the bow downstream.

With a gush, the spring current took control, but Jim had been in heavy water before. So he used the 10-inch blade of the ash paddle to rudder the craft; content to let the flow do the work. In no time at all, he had been propelled pass the outlet of Johnson Stream; *for a small brook, it sure has plenty of runoff,* Jim observed. In a little under two hours, the ranger had floated out of the upper stream and into Allagash Lake.

The flying service had been right. The north shore of the lake was free of ice to an area beyond Sandy Point campsite, a considerable distance. To his right, the water was navigable for about 200 yards after which a solid white frozen mini-glacier blocked the way to camp, and to the outboard motor and canoe that waited.

The ranger quickly surveyed the lake. He

counted a total of ten canoes. Eight were on the lake fishing, and the other two were beached at Ledge Point. Everything seemed normal so the voyager headed to camp.

Jim paddled across the open water, and when he reached the white mass, the ranger ran the canoe rocker as far as possible onto the solid ice. He was going to have to get out and walk. Without standing, he then grabbed his pole ax and cut a hole in the frozen surface. The ice appeared to be about four inches thick.

Then very carefully he stood, bent at the waist and grabbed both gunwales. Gingerly, Jim then placed his right foot on the hard surface beside the canoe. The ice held. The ranger then, still gripping the canoe, slid his left foot beside his right onto the slippery surface. Jim then pulled the canoe farther onto the ice until he could stand behind the stern deck, on solid ice. The man then bent over with his hands on the nearest thwart and pushed the canoe, one step at a time, toward the south shore and safety.

Jim was halfway across the ice when his right foot broke through, immediately his boot filled with slushy lake water. Jim threw himself onto the canoe, the craft rocked onto its starboard side but then settled back onto the frozen surface.

The experienced woodsman pulled his foot out of the water, once again found solid footing, and continued pushing the canoe. When he got closer to shore, Jim saw that the ice had retreated from the stone beach and left 70 feet of open water between him and safety. Nearing the edge of the ice, Jim seated himself back into the canoe, and using his canoe pole thrust the canoe over the edge of the ice and into blue water.

The canoe, once again at home, held steady and with one foot soaked, Jim paddled the remaining distance to the rocky shore. When the bow touched land, Jim climbed out of the canoe, and turned to look back at where he had broken through. The hole his foot had created was already several inches wide, *must be a spring hole there*; the ranger thought and then dismissed the experience now that he was safe.

Relieved to be on firm footing, Jim set the bow of the canoe on shore and carried his gear to camp. Jim unlocked the door, built a wood fire, and changed out of his wet clothes. Once comfortable, he remembered to check the time. It had taken exactly two hours and fifty-five minutes to get from the truck to camp; he'd better radio the boss.

Leigh had paced around his office for two hours and fifty-seven minutes when he heard...

"1703 to 1700."

Relieved, the supervisor grabbed the microphone, ignored the language of the official ten code and said, "Go ahead, Jim."

"Everything is fine. I am at camp."

"That's good news, Jim. Thank you. Can you see if there is much ice left in the lake?"

"10-4, there is. Quite a bit in front of camp. But the wind is starting to pick up and so if the ice floe gets blown around much, I suspect break up will occur at any time."

"Many on the lake?"

"From what I can tell there are about six parties with about 20 people," Jim reported and continued, "I'll check on them as soon as I can get free."

"10-4, Jim. Let me know how the place wintered when you have a chance to look around." And with that Supervisor Leigh Smith put down the radio mike, picked up the phone, and called the flying service to let them know they wouldn't be needed, for now. Back on Allagash Lake—the wind picked up!

*****

Jim thought the camp was going to blow over! The wind gradually increased the rest of the day. After getting propane turned on and gear stored, he had spent the afternoon preparing his canoe, motor, and chainsaw for when the lake became navigable. That night Jim made a supper of baked ham with pineapple, mashed potatoes, biscuits, topped off with chocolate cake and fresh brewed coffee. After dishes, he read the latest nonfiction best seller.

Shortly after 9 P.M. the blasts from the northwest turned into a full fledge twister. A deep breathing, spinning circle of wind as 'lady spring' battled 'ole man winter' *in a fight to the finish* for control of the frozen kingdom. To the northwest thunder rolled like an approaching locomotive through distance skies.

The ranger's camp creaked, groaned, and snapped in protest; but the board and batten building stood its ground. The windows of the three-room cabin rattled in the 40-mile per hour onslaught, and an invisible hand forced open the porch's screen door with a bang.

With such a tempest, Jim worried that his canoes might get blown away, so before going to bed he'd gone outside and slid his Grumman and Traveler under the camp. Before returning inside there was another sound. Resounding from deep in the forest, echoed crashing sounds of the wind snapping trees like matchsticks. Shutting off his propane lights, Jim climbed into bed and planned for the next day, *good thing the chainsaw is running–sounds like I'm gonna need it.* But not a stick of softwood fell near camp.

By 2 A.M. the gale had blown itself out. At daylight Jim walked down to the shore; surveyed the damage and saw the rolling waves of a crystal blue lake, fully ice free. To the south and east, broken cakes of ice littered the shoreline.

After the intense storm, Jim decided to check on the campers at the campsites across the way. In the canoe, Jim motored toward the Ledges. When he was about 200 yards out, a man ran to shore, hollered and waved at the ranger. Jim couldn't hear over the noise of the outboard, but sensing an emergency he approached the Ledge Point campsite at double speed. Running the bow of his aluminum canoe onto the pea stone landing, Jim turned off the Mercury outboard motor, jumped onto shore, and set the canoe solidly onto the beach.

Immediately the waiting man instructed, "Come quick—**come quick I tell you!**"

"What's the matter?" the ranger asked?

"We think our friend is having a heart attack." The man fretfully explained, "The symptoms started yesterday after you crossed the lake, we saw you almost fall in. We couldn't get your attention. Oh crap, I hope he'll be ok!"

"Try and relax. It's better if your friend sees that you've remained calm." Jim coolly suggested. "Let me take a look and we'll see what can be done."

Walking across the campsite, the man led Jim to the third tent in line. Four men sat around a picnic table, looking helpless.

"He's in here, please hurry," the frantic leader begged as he unzipped the nylon door of the four-person tent.

Peering inside, Jim saw a puffy faced man lying inside a sleeping bag, his skin was ash gray and there were beads of cold sweat on his forehead. "Hi there, my name is Jim. I'm the ranger on the lake and I've come to see how you are doing." Jim said so casually anyone listening would have thought they were discussing the best place to net a trout.

Panting, the victim replied, "I don't know. I just don't know. Yesterday I felt ok before lunch. I'd spent most of the morning cutting and splitting firewood. But

I slipped off the ledge and fell into the water when I tried to get water to heat for dishes. God, the lake was cold. Then I started getting chest pains." The man gasped, searched for breath and asked, ""You got a cigarette? I sure could use a light." When Jim didn't reply the man continued, "Then I got heartburn, sick to my stomach, and my arms hurt real bad. And gosh my sleeping bag and I are soaking wet with perspiration."

With a weak hand he touched Jim's forearm and faintly asked, "Am I going to die?"

From the diary of James Clark
Evacuation

This is my second night back on Allagash Lake for the summer. The trip down the stream was fast and across the ice pack in front of camp was, interesting.

Last night a heavy wind came through and cleared the last of the ice from the lake. This morning I had the first emergency evacuation of the summer. A man on Ledge Point campsite had all of the symptoms of a heart attack. His party had contemplated taking their friend by canoe back up the stream and to their vehicles parked at the upper put-in.

Thank goodness I arrived when I did. With the amount of water coming down the upper stream, a healthy man with an empty canoe would have had a hard time. Going up the stream loaded, hauling a sick man would have been impossible.

Upon examination, I learned that the patient was about 40 years, he appeared moderately overweight, and that he was taking medication for high blood pressure and cholesterol. His friends said he'd been under extreme stress at work and smoked a pack and a half of cigarettes a day.

I knew it didn't look good for the man but I assured the victim he wasn't going to die. Then I radioed the department's Greenville dispatch and asked them to contact Roger at Currier's Flying Service. They were to convey I had an individual exhibiting signs of a heart attack; and that we needed a plane to land on Allagash Lake for transport. I then confirmed that I'd meet the aircraft at the ledge campsite.

Within minutes, dispatch radioed back that the plane was on the way in with two EMTs. In about 45 minutes we saw a red and white Cessna 180 with silver pontoons circle the lake. After ensuring the landing zone was safe the aircraft landed into the wind and taxied up to the campsite.

While the EMTs took the vital signs of the sick man, I helped Roger turn the 180 so the tail of the floats were anchored on shore. We then removed the right hand door and folded down the back of the right front and rear seats. By now the medics had stabilized the victim and wrapped him in a blanket. He was then strapped into an aluminum stretcher and made ready to load into the plane.

Four of us slid the stretcher diagonally over the wing strut, and over the right and rear seats. The foot of the stretcher extended into the extended baggage compartment. The head of the stretcher positioned directly behind the back of the front seat. One EMT sat on the folded rear seat, beside the sufferer and the other caregiver in the front right seat.

With the whole party hollering

"Good luck," come back in soon." We're here for another four days," with a throaty cough, the engine of the aircraft started and the rescue vehicle moved away from shore.

The loaded plane taxied for about a half a mile, turned into the wind, and under full power, lifted one pontoon slightly off the lake to break surface tension, and took off for the Greenville hospital.

Once the scene was secure, I turned to the leader and inquired about the victim's name and he replied, "Its Mark, Mark Fraser from Bangor." Once they had provided all of the information needed for my reports, I told the party I'd let 'em know if I learned the diagnosis for their friend. I spent the rest of the day patrolling the lake, and removing blowdowns from the campsites. I hope Mark will be ok.

*****

The next morning Jim was getting ready to motor down to the Carry Trail at the south end of the lake when his two-way radio came to life.

"Greenville to 1703."

"10-3, Greenville.""Currier's called and they have heard from the Charles A. Dean Memorial Hospital. Roger said to tell you that Mark, the man evacuated yesterday **had been** having a heart attack, but the doctors got to him in time. His arteries are clogged, but they are operating today, and the prognosis is very good."

"10-4, Greenville, that's good news. Please thank Currier's Flying Service for the quick work and excellent response."

An hour later...

Jim returned to the Ledges campsite, and five guys were seated and staring unseeing at the empty fireplace, worried about the condition of their friend. Jim beached his canoe, and approached the group. The men looked up with wary anticipation; anxious but still not sure they wanted to hear what the ranger had to say. "I've heard from the hospital and the doctors advised that Mark is going to recover. He'll need surgery, but they sent word that he'll be ok and will meet you back home."

Immediately the five men, very relieved for their friend, broke out in a loud "Thank god!" and then happily cheered, laughed, and patted each other on the back.

After a moment of celebration, the men turned to thank Jim for the rescue, but he was gone. A half a mile out on the lake a ranger, the brim of his cap pulled low against the intensity of the morning sun, sat in a 20-foot canoe and motored slowly and scanned the lake for anything unusual; *because a ranger just never knows when a situation might come to call.*

*****

*Author's Note 1: In April of 1983 gusts of wind up to 40 miles per hour were recorded in Maine. That April, a northwest blast roared across a frozen Chamberlain Lake with such force, that it drove slabs of lake ice into the shore in front of Nugent's Camps. The power of the tempest plowed up several feet of shoreline and lifted the front of a number of lakefront buildings as high as four feet in the air.

April 29, 1983 Damage to one of Nugent's camps.

**Author's Note 2: In April of 1984 there was so much snow and ice packed into the trail around Allagash Falls, that rangers had to cut a route through a frozen glacier so spring paddlers could portage around the Falls.

Ranger Lee Hafford is standing center of the opened pathway.

Lee Hafford at Allagash Falls. Photograph from the Tim Caverly collection.

Reader's Notes:

21
GONE

Arriving at Pleasant Ridge early Monday morning as Jim had asked; Margaret encountered an ambulance with flashing red and blue emergency lights that had pulled up to the doors of the assisted living community. She pulled into her usual parking spot and noticed the space where the 4x4 was normally parked, was now empty. The correspondent had most of the material she needed for the newspaper article and now wanted to ask a couple of clarification questions, and thank Jim for his time.

Her assignment was nearly complete, but Margaret hoped to keep the diaries a while longer just in case she wanted to double check her facts, if her new found friend would let her.

Walking to the entrance there was a flurry of activity. A bustle of doctors, nurses, and orderlies were packing medical bags and rushing out of the building while residents gathered in small clusters and whispered in low tones.

Walking to the desk, the receptionist looked up at Margaret's approach. From the redness of the greeter's eyes, the reporter could tell she'd been crying. "Is Jim here?" the journalist asked.

The greeter waited a minute before she replied, took a deep breath and sniveled, "We think Jim is gone. The ambulance has taken him away and George has followed the hospital vehicle with the family truck."

Feeling like she had been slapped, Margaret couldn't believe what she was hearing. *It couldn't be true! He'd seemed so healthy at her last visit.* "What happened?" the writer said as she felt the weight of sadness in the room and collapsed into the nearest chair.

"Jim's son was visiting and his boy said his father started complaining of chest pains and that his left arm was numb. We called the fire department and they sent an ambulance to transport Jim. It happened so sudden. Just yesterday he'd told some of his stories in the game room; we were all there laughing. I don't know, I just don't know. So sad—so sad!"

Margaret rose to her feet, but her knees felt weak like they couldn't support the weight of the sorrow and were going to buckle at any minute. Struggling to find the composure she didn't feel; Margaret wandered unseeing into the dayroom. There the puzzle lady said to Margaret, "We are so sorry. He spoke so well of you. Jim said you were like family. We all are going to miss him. Yes, all of us for sure!"

Margaret forced a smile and looked about the area filled with residents. She noticed that the coffee pot was empty, several types of birds had disappeared from the feeder, and a cloud blocked the sun, preventing the day's warmth from flowing into the usually cheerful room. Everywhere Margaret looked there was the feeling of emptiness. Maggie could feel that a strange quiet had settled like a silencing fog over the community. Residents were sitting all about. Those who were talking were doing so in soft whispers out of respect for a missing friend.

Others were just sitting about and watching the remaining birds that remained perched outside in nature's harmony a few sang and ignored the well-stocked feeders. Margaret thought that the melody of the winged friends seemed especially soothing today, like the sweetness of a heavenly refrain. Returning to the entrance she saw that Jim's chair was positioned as before, only this time it was empty. Despite the room being crowded and many stood, no one claimed the vacant seat.

After a while Margaret regained her composure and wandered down to Jim's room. The door was unlocked and she felt strangely uncomfortable entering a place where she had spent so much time, but she felt or *was it needed* to take one last visit to–*a home away from home*, she thought *a place I felt relaxed, safe, and welcome.*

Walking by the bathroom door into the living area, everything was there. The pictures and award plaques on the wall, the decorated cookstove, and the stuffed deer mount. Margaret couldn't quite tell, everything seemed to be there but yet *something was absent.*

Margaret noticed that the middle drawer to the desk was opened and so she decided to close it before leaving the room. *What's missing?* The reporter wondered as she approached the desk. Putting her hand on the drawer's handle, she noticed an envelope sitting in a place of prominence, where it would be readily seen. Intending to push the correspondence inside the desk drawer she saw bold handwriting that identified the addressee: To Margaret Woodward following by the instructions, If I am not here, please see that Ms. Woodward gets this envelope. And it was signed Thank you. James Paul Clark

Moving the letter, Margaret noticed there were several nearly full bottles of medicine. Reading the labels, the prescriptions were made out to Jim and were prescribed to lower cholesterol and drop his blood pressure. *If these are Jim's meds, it sure seems like he didn't take many. Wonder if that is what got him?*

He had left her a note, perhaps his final words? Margaret wondered as she caressed the handwriting to make one final connection with her friend.

Margaret tucked the envelope in her coat pocket, closed the drawer, and walked toward the hall. Taking one last look at the mounted deer head, Margaret understood what had disappeared. *It was the Marlin rifle, the 38-40,* she thought. Then Margaret assumed that *probably the son took it.*

Getting into her car, Margaret didn't open the letter right off, but decided to drive back to her apartment so she could read her friend's words in privacy. She was still choking back the tears, and wasn't sure how much longer she could hold back the flood of sadness that consumed her body. It was like she had once again, lost her family.

Once inside her apartment and seated at her favorite spot by the window, Margaret poured an extra strong cup of coffee, opened the letter, only to have a small key fall out of the envelope and bounce onto the floor by her feet. Picking up the key and holding it with her left hand Margaret read the typed pages:

May 29th

Dear Maggie,

THIS IS FOR YOUR EYES ONLY! Please keep this message confidential.

I didn't want to leave without saying goodbye. I've only stayed at the center these many years because I was waiting for your visit and ask about my time in the woods. I've had a good life and one that I thought others might enjoy. I also hope that someday my experiences will be of interest to my family. But I needed the right person to write that story. Your editor, Mark, said he thought that you were the one. And as we talked I knew you were the person in the image I saw on the walls of the Ice Caves so many years ago.

As a young man I wished I had asked my mom, dad, and grandfather about our family history but never got around to it. I suspect that my sons and daughter will feel the same way someday, and when that time comes, your article will be a family treasure.

I've enjoyed speaking with you these last few weeks and I wish you good luck with your career as a newspaper reporter. I am convinced you'll do well. You are very smart and I suspect you've already figured out that I am not as helpless as the nurses and others have tried to make me. It was easier to go along rather than argue and by allowing them to think me so; made for an easier getaway for when it came the time to leave.

You may remember that early on in our conversation I told you that the old tan–colored pickup in the parking lot was nothing more than as a psychological aid so I would feel that I could go home. The facility told me they kept the key so I wouldn't lose it. But I know they did it to prevent me from leaving. What the home doesn't know is that I've had a spare key ever since I've been here; and have been waiting for the right moment to pack the vehicle. My son has been getting the truck ready for me and the home thinks the truck is his to keep.

Now that we've chatted and the alder leafs are as big as a mouse's ear it is time for me to go fishing and return to the woods where I belong. Don't try to find me because you won't be able to. But if you happen to paddle into Allagash Lake and set up camp at the Ledges campsite, don't be surprised if early some morning or the last thing before dark, you see an old gent with a golden retriever in a green canoe, catching brookies out of a spring hole in a bogan that lies south of where the inlet marries the lake.

The enclosed key is to my grandfather's old trunk. The only members of my family who know about the old chest are my wife Susan and daughter Isabella. I never told my sons because they would have opened it, and I wanted you to be the one to find the heirlooms inside. My wife and daughter promised to respect my wishes to save the chest for you. Isabella will tell you where it is kept. Bella can be reached by calling her cellphone, the number is at the bottom of this letter. Once you open the luggage, you'll understand why I saved the valuables for you.

When you are done with my treasures, keep what you need and return the rest to my daughter. She knows what to do with the collection.

Goodbye and I wish you good health and much success.

Fondly,

Jim

James P. Clark

Reader's Notes:

AFTERWORD

A man walked across the platform to take his place behind a lectern on center stage. Attired in a tuxedo, the speaker scanned the elegantly decorated banquet room while he waited for the well-dressed audience to quiet. Looking over the crowd he estimated that there had to be at least 300 television and radio personalities seated around circular tables strategically placed to ensure optimum viewing of the rostrum.

The ornamental room was adorned with dining tables embellished with linen table cloths, vases of brightly colored flowers, crystal wine glasses, china plates and cups flanked by a full setting of silverware. The allotted time for the evening's ceremony was drawing to a close. For the most part, all of the attendees had finished their selected four-course feasts of poached Atlantic salmon or prime rib. Even the most casual observer could tell that tonight was a very festive occasion.

The Master of Ceremonies, and last speaker for the evening, spoke into the microphone and said **"Good Evening, my name is Scott Fletcher and I am President and CEO of the New England Broadcasting Company. Welcome ladies and**

gentlemen to the Annual Congress of New England Journalists." After receiving polite applause he looked directly at the members of the audience and continued in a voice polished by years of working on the air.

"Tonight as you know we are gathered to celebrate the success of one of our own. You, my fellow journalists, have responded well to our survey to determine New England's Correspondent of the Year. Here the speaker was greeted by an even louder ovation. After the clapping subsided he continued…

"It was a difficult decision with a field of over 25 of colleagues nominated. Tonight's recipient will receive this coveted NCNEA plaque, an all-expense paid, seven- day stay at Maine's own Johnson's Allagash Lodge, and $5,000 in cash." Here audience once again erupted, but the speaker continued, **"The candidate selected has demonstrated the highest excellence in journalism. This person was evaluated on their precision, the depth and breadth of their accuracy, and if their piece was of a fair and balanced style. And last, but not least, if their work engaged their readers.**

"We are pleased to announce that this

evening's winner is also being awarded the prestigious American Literary Award for Excellence. An honor that guarantees a book contract with an advance of $10,000."

The audience gasped and then broke into a roaring, handclapping ovation. Everyone in the room expected and hoped that they were going to be chosen.

Then in an even louder voice, the MC announced, **"without further ado, tonight's selected recipient is…"** he paused briefly for effect and then loudly announced **"Margaret Sanborn Woodward for her feature Our Maine Man-The story of Ranger James Paul Clark, published by the Penobscot Basin Times of Bangor, Maine."**

Thunderous applause echoed throughout the room and 299 people immediately stood and turned to look and smile directly at Margaret who sat speechless, red-faced, and embarrassed.

Stunned, unbelieving, Maggie subconsciously clenched the copper coin necklace fastened around her neck. The reporter remained frozen until her editor, sitting beside her, smiling, gave his reporter a nudge and whispered loud enough for her to hear over the crowd—"Get up Margaret, get up! They are waiting on stage for you to go up and receive the awards."

EPILOGUE

Maggie emerges from the upper stream and paddles her dark gray craft across the calm water of Allagash Lake. Once beyond influence of the Inlet's flow, she turns her canoe slightly to the north and sculls towards the Ledges campsite. This is her first visit to the wilderness corridor and she is thrilled by the stillness and the natural beauty which surrounds her. She has come in search of a friend and prays that he is ok.

Early each morning she sits on the ledges along the shore and uses field glasses to scan the lake. Of particular importance is a nearby bayou where she watches for any sign of a fisherman and a golden retriever fishing from the popular Atkinson Traveler. Seeing no one, the woman spends her days exploring the lake from her own canoe. Activities such as hiking the trail to the lookout tower on the top of 1,809-foot Allagash Mountain. There she picks fresh blueberries and gazes at the world below. Mesmerized by the view, she feels insignificant against the backdrop of a blue sky and acres of dark green forest.

Leaving the mountain, the single paddler moves her canoe easily across a flat calm lake. Arriving at the pond's outlet, she guides "the 18-foot canoe around the remains of an old roll logging dam; a remembrance of when thousands of cords floated down tributaries and streams toward paper and lumber mills located over a hundred miles away.

Caught by the current, she quickly covers the three miles down the lake's lower stream to Little Allagash Falls. There she devours a tuna sandwich and studies the potholes in the blue-gray ledges worn years before by small stones held captive in the washed out stone hollows. Once encased, the rocks had spun like in washing machine fashion– around and around –potholing bigger and bigger cavities whenever spring floods cascaded over the outcroppings.

Wading upstream through shallow water, the adventurer pulls on the canoe's bow line until she reaches water deep enough to paddle. Arriving back on the expanse of blue water the lady is tired so she blades the streamline boat to an expansive sand beach on the north end of the 4,000 acre lake. There she takes a natural sunbath, secure in the feeling that she has the lake to *herself*. Refreshed, she paddles to the famous Ice Caves where Maggie descends deep into the caverns to look for any indication of etchings that may have once been scribed on the granite walls well below ground, but she doesn't find any.

Each day before dark the lady arrives back at the campsite where she takes up a vigil of watching and waiting for her friend to appear. But he never does. After five days it is time to return to her desk at the Times. *Maybe*, she thinks, *my editor will allow me time to work on my book about the river. I can't help but sense that there is a much bigger story here! And it's time for me to search out Bella, and find the trunk. What could possibly be stored in that luggage? s*he wonders and then considers *I hate to leave, this would be a great place to spend the summer working on a book.*

On the last night of the camping trip, the reporter makes a final trek to the 'Caves'. Standing in opening of this ancient chasm she removes a penny amulet threaded onto to a blue nylon necklace. Margaret gently drapes the charm over a softwood root that grows over the center of the cavern's entrance. Watching for a moment, the lady turned to walk down the trail. Twenty feet down the path, within sight of the cave, she pauses at the base of a large standing white birch tree and, with an indelible sharpie marker she carries for just such an occasion; Margaret scribes in black ink a final homage to her friend; The Ranger and the Reporter–*if he is still alive, maybe Jim will see it?*

Tomorrow she'll return home and to her future husband, and wait for a son yet to be born. Secure in the knowledge that the lucky charm, delivered by her great uncle, will patiently wait until someday another person will escape to the woods to retrieve the coin *for the sake of the family*. Within minutes the one-cent talisman fades invisibly into the stone over the moss covered fissure, but the ink on the tree remained.

Back at the Ledges campsite Maggie watched the campfire until the flames died. Once the hot embers had turned from red to black, she walked toward the tent and to bed. From somewhere out in the lake a loon called and the ancient's bird's tremolos was promptly answered by a "barred owl inquiring "who cooks for you?" Hearing the question, she softly wonders *what must it be like for the wives of woodsman, like Susan Clark, who lived in the remote forest with their warden and ranger husbands? How did the women handle the isolation, when the men were away? Did the ladies miss their moms, dads and families back home? Or* Margaret pondered, *was constantly worrying if their spouse would return in one piece– a greater fear?*

The stars were so bright Margaret felt like she could pluck one from the sky and take it home. Crawling into her nylon shelter and wiggling into a goose down sleeping bag, the journalist sighs softly with disappointment because she hasn't found her friend. Maggie immediately falls asleep and into the deepest slumber she has had in years.

Early the next morning she woken to the sound of a crackling fire and briefly considers making coffee, only coming fully alert when she remembers that the night before she had extinguished the campfire.

Worried there might be a wildfire, Maggie threw off her bedding and flew out the door of the tent. Once in the open air she is relieved to discover a small warming fire burning brightly in the site's rocked up fireplace. Curious as to how the blaze could have started, the lady walks towards the warm glow.

When she passes the cedar picnic table she discovers someone has left her breakfast. A pint jar of canned fiddleheads and a large, brook trout, rolled in cornmeal, lying on a piece of light tan birch bark that waits to be cooked. On the table, beside the morning meal, she found a note written on the white side of a smaller piece of the paper-like tree skin. Picking up the pastoral note, she discovers a message written in charcoal, by someone who'd used the small end of a burnt hardwood twig, like a pencil.

Thinking *my, the handwriting looks strangely familiar* Maggie reads:

Dear Maggie,

I hope you enjoy breakfast.

I am well and trust you are to. By the way I hear a ranger's job has opened on the lake and the Department will be interviewing soon.

Don't forget the trunk!

I remain fondly yours,

Stunned by this note and the early morning gifts, Margaret looked up, directly at the inlet. There she saw the distant silhouette of a person and a dog in a canoe fade into the morning fog. Looking back down at the note she rereads the last sentence **"a job has opened on the lake and the Department of Conservation will be interviewing soon!"**

Matt LaRoche with 31-inch, 11 pound lake trout
Photograph from the Matt LaRoche Collection.

Epitaph

(Written at Allagash Lake from the Ledge campsite one July
evening.)

The lake was calm
And the night was still.
I rested alone,
Absorbing my fill;

Of clean air and trees
and warm summer breeze.
When near my feet
I did see;

Some carved lettering
There-just below!
Marks in stone,
Carved long ago.

By visitors who'd walked this ground
Long before;
Where I sit today,
Just above the shore.

Initials and dates made note;
By others such as I;
Who treasured this ground
From Where they watched,
The years fly by.

The marks weren't meant
To be graffiti, or to deface
But as a simple reflection of appreciation;
for this special place.

These letters in stone
Brought a message to my ear,
Just to let me know that
"Someone was here."

Jim Clark
T8R14, Maine

THIS BOOK HAS RECEIVED THE GOLDEN RETRIEVER AND MOTHER-IN-LAW DARN GOOD READING' AWARD

Sunfire's Allagash Sand aka Sandi
Photograph from the Tim Caverly Collection.

Sandi critiqued "I recommend The Ranger and the Reporter because the story makes me want to go for a walk in the woods."

Joan King in uniform.|

Photograph from the Tim Caverly Collection.

Joan the mother-in-law said, "I applaud this story because it reminded me of when I lived in the woods and I can't wait to go back."

**Be sure to check out our full line of products
from the**
ALLAGASH TAILS COLLECTION

VISIT US ONLINE AT
WWW.ALLAGASHTAILS.COM

Tim and Sandi the Golden Retriever at Gull Rock (Please forgive the helmet hair)—Chamberlain Lake, April 2015

TIM'S BIO...

Tim Caverly is a Maine author who has written and published seven books about Maine's northern forest. In addition, several of Tim's short stories have been printed in newspapers, magazines and outdoor journals. His second book "An Allagash Haunting" has been adapted into a stage play and performed numerous times.

Through their "New England Reads" literacy project, Tim and Frank Manzo Jr. had, by 2015 provided 157 power point programs to almost 6,000 students. In addition, to encourage literacy and learning about New England's natural world, they have donated over 1500 Allagash Tail's books to 133 New England schools.

Due to accompanying his fire warden dad and ranger brother 'on patrol' and his 32 years as a Maine Park Ranger; Tim has lived in the four corners of Maine. Readers can depend that his stories are based on personal experiences and knowledge of our state's history and landscapes.

Frank shares his love of art with his daughter Bella.
Photo by Gabriel Manzo

FRANK'S BIO...

Frank was born and raised in Millinocket, Maine where he attended Stearns High School. After working as a software engineer for over 25 years, he returned to his family homestead in his hometown. Frank is a noted artist and his photographs and illustrations are popular and enjoyed by all. Frank's prior work experiences includes; editor of a local newspaper, teaching in the Millinocket School System and he is currently a Database Specialist at Eastern Maine Medical Centers in the center's Performance Improvement, Data Management Department.

Frank has always enjoyed pursuing art and sharing his drawings with his children. He is an avid hiker, camper, and outdoorsman and enjoys being able to share his love of the North Maine Woods by illustrating for Allagash Tails.